the spice of life

A cross-curricular approach to food and cookery for children from five to eleven

Kay Dunbar

Displays by Katie Kitching

Illustrations by Sally Stiff

First published in 1992 by
BELAIR PUBLICATIONS LIMITED
P.O. Box 12, Twickenham, England, TW1 2QL

© Kay Dunbar
Series Editor Robyn Gordon
Designed by Richard Souper
Photography by Kelvin Freeman
Typesetting by Belair
Printed and Bound in Hong Kong by World Print Ltd
ISBN 0 947882 19 7

Acknowledgements

The author and publishers would like to thank the children, parents and staff at Park School, Dartington, Devon; and at Buckland Infants School, Chessington, Kingston-upon-Thames, for their contributions and generous support. They would also like to to give thanks for cover artwork to Meryl Gray (aged 7).

Contents

Introduction

Learning about all aspects of food and cooking has limitless fascination for most children and can be approached from many aspects of the curriculum.

Cooking is particularly pleasurable but may be considered difficult to organise in class. However, despite large classes and small classrooms, it is still possible to find a way. For some teachers the best system is to arrange for parents to take a small group aside for cooking activities. While it is invaluable having extra help on these occasions, I feel many learning opportunities may be missed if the teacher does not have an active role in the cookery lessons. The teacher can encourage the children to think, plan, predict, observe, describe and compare.

Why do we need to wet the edges of the pastry?
What does the dough feel like?
Where do lemons come from?
What will happen if we don't add eggs to the mixture?

Some recipes lend themselves to whole class activities by dividing the class into groups and each group being responsible for one part of the recipe. Vast quantities of vegetable soup, for instance, can be produced by one group being in charge of potato peeling, one group washing leeks, one group chopping celery etc.

In this book there are many other activities related to food in addition to cooking, so one group could be cooking while others are working on a related activity. For instance, one group could be making elderflower cordial while another is drawing the elderflowers, another designing labels for bottles etc.

The organisation of cookery lessons will be less difficult if the teacher establishes routines which ensure order and efficiency. This is true of all lessons but particularly helpful in making cookery lessons run smoothly. Time spent at the outset instilling good habits saves time and chaos later. Most important, of course, is safety. Cookery can mean hot dishes, sharp knives, germs, electricity. It sounds daunting but need not be. The secret is to anticipate any potential danger and make safety rules in advance. Children always respond best to rules they have helped to make themselves, so discuss with them any likely hazards and let them formulate the necessary guidelines.

Some of the recipes here may seem to be unusual choices for children but they have been chosen because they are interesting to study rather than because they are favourite foods. You will be surprised how adventurous children will be when they have cooked something themselves. Just a small taste of some dishes is all that is required for the experience. Few children will want more than a small sip of xocolatl (drinking chocolate) when it is made the Aztec way. There are exceptions however. The main aim has been to present a selection of delicious recipes, and I feel sure that they will be very popular, besides providing the stimulus for varied learning experiences.

Kay Dunbar
1992

Hedgerow Cookery and Seasonal Foods

Paintings of elderflowers on circular black paper, displayed with elderflower cordial recipe and relevant vocabulary

Discussion

Which foods do children eat that are seasonal? Most foods are available now all year round. Why is this? Are there times of the year when there is a surplus of particular types of food? This is sometimes called a glut.

Activities

Make a wheel showing the four seasons and write about, draw or paint the fruit and vegetables which are grown in each season in this country.

Language

Read the poem 'The Calendar' by Barbara Euphan Todd in *I Like This Poem,* edited by Kaye Webb, Puffin. Each verse deals with one of the four seasons. Using her poem as a model, ask the children to write a poem with each verse beginning 'I knew when Spring had come' (Summer, Autumn, Winter). This activity would be suitable for collaborative writing in groups of 3 or 4 children. Each group could write about a season and they could be put together to make a class poem. Also as a group activity, the children could appoint a scribe to make a large copy of their verse which the rest could illustrate. The four seasons together would make a poster poem.

ELDER

Elder is a common hedgerow shrub. The creamy white blossom opens in May and has a heady scent. The tiny black berries appear in early autumn and last for several weeks, if the birds do not eat them. Blackbirds are particularly fond of elderberries.

ALICE ASTOR'S ELDERFLOWER CORDIAL
About a week before you are going to make cordial, show the children some elder twigs. Ask them to look carefully at the flower clusters and at the leaves. Smell the flowers. Explain that you are going to make the cordial from an *infusion* of the flowers, i.e. the flowers are placed in a liquid in order to extract the flavour. Ask the children to collect some flower heads themselves if possible.

Recipe
Makes approx 1 litre of *concentrated* cordial

1 litre (1¾ pt) water
1½ kg (3¼ lb) sugar
1 sliced lemon
75g (3oz) citric acid
20 heads of elderflower

Bring water to the boil. Add sugar and lemon. Remove from heat and stir until the sugar is dissolved. Reboil and add the citric acid and flowerheads. Leave until cool and then strain the liquid. Bottle. Dilute to taste. The children could drink the cordial themselves or share with other children at break, or the school could have an elderflower cordial stall at the Summer Fair.

Art
● Paint pictures of the flowerheads. Mix the paint carefully to match the cream colour
  of the flowers. Black paper is most effective. These could be displayed together
  with the recipe for the cordial and the relevant vocabulary. (See photograph.)
● Draw the flowerheads with fine black pens.
● Use coloured pencils for delicate flower drawings.

ELDERBERRY JELLY
If you have made elderflower cordial in the spring, you will know where to find the elderberries in the autumn. Stripping the berries off the stems is laborious work, but it keeps the whole class busy. You can introduce the proverb 'Many hands make light work'!

Recipe
1kg (2¼ lb) (approx) elderberries
600ml (1pt) water
1kg (2¼ lb) sugar - for each litre (1¾ pts) of juice produced

Bring water and fruit to the boil. Simmer until the fruit is soft, keeping the hot liquid well away from the children. Secure a jelly bag or a pillowcase to a chair, pour in the cooked elderberries and let it strain overnight into a bucket. In the morning there will be thick red juice in the bucket. Let the children taste the liquid at this stage. (Remove a small amount of juice into a bowl for this purpose.)
Measure the liquid. For each litre (1¾ pts) of juice add 1kg (2¼ lb) of sugar. Dissolve the sugar over a low heat. Boil vigorously until it reaches setting point. To test for setting, put a small amount of the jelly onto a saucer and let it cool. If it wrinkles it is ready. Cool slightly and then pot. **N.B. For all preserving recipes it is necessary to wash and dry the pots carefully and then to warm them in an oven before filling.**

Art
● Design the labels. Use large sticky labels to give more space for decoration.

MINT
There are many different kinds of mint: apple mint, lemon mint, catmint etc. In the following recipes I am referring to spearmint, which is the most common mint. Ask the children to name some products which include mint flavourings.

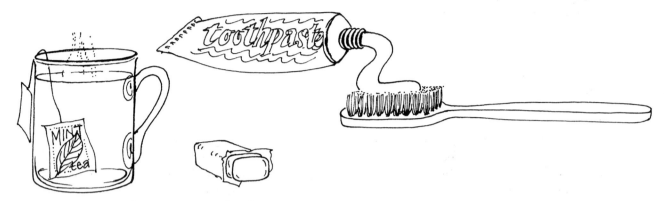

mint tea, spearmint-flavoured toothpaste and indigestion tablets

Gardening
Children may not realise that spearmint is a plant. Give each child a mint to suck and a mint leaf to taste to introduce them to the herb mint. Ask them to name other products that are flavoured with mint. It is very easy to grow mint; a few roots will soon spread and fill a container. Cuttings can be taken from a friend's plant, or the herb bought from a garden centre. Plant rooted runners in deep, rich soil. Keep in a shady position until early spring. Cut back regularly to encourage fresh growth.

MINT SAUCE

Recipe
Lots of finely chopped mint (young children could use scissors)
For every 4 tablespoons of mint add 1 teaspoon of sugar
2 tablespoons of lemon juice
4 teaspoons boiling water
1 tablespoon white wine vinegar
Mix all the ingredients together and allow to cool. The classroom will be filled with pungent smells. Fill small jars with the mint sauce.

Art
Write and decorate the labels for jars of mint sauce. These would make good Summer Fair products if you have an excess.

Hedgerow Cookery and Seasonal Foods

STRAWBERRIES

Strawberries remain a relatively seasonal fruit as they do not freeze very well.

A visit to a 'Pick Your Own' strawberry farm is very popular with children and the costs can be offset by having a strawberry sale. When organising an outing it is most effective to involve the children at all stages of the planning.

- Look in the local paper with the class to find the address of a 'Pick Your Own' farm.
- As a class activity, compose a letter to the farmer asking if you may visit his farm. Discuss with the children what he will need to know: date, time of arrival, number of children etc. Explain about stamped, addressed envelopes and enclose one with the letter.
- Show the children the correct way to set out letters and address envelopes.
- The day before the visit, phone the farmer to check on the state, quantity and price of the strawberries. These can be variable, depending on the weather.
- As the children can pick with enthusiasm, the strawberry bill can be vast. To pay for this, allow children to buy strawberries themselves, if they wish, at the farm price and then have a strawberry stall at school at the end of the day for teachers and parents. Aim to make a small profit to help pay for your day out.

- If you still have any strawberries left you could make the following recipe.

STRAWBERRY SORBET
Makes enough for everyone in a class of 30 to have a taste

300g (11oz) sugar
600ml (1 pt) water
750g (1¾ lb) strawberries (soft fruit is ideal)
1 egg white

Heat the water and dissolve the sugar in it and let it cool. Press the strawberries through a sieve and stir them into the water. Freeze for 3-4 hours, removing the mixture every half hour to whisk. After one hour stiffly whisk the egg white and add to strawberry mixture. Leave in the freezer until needed. Serve a little to each child as an end of day treat.

APPLES

By September/October it is usually possible to find people who are desperate to get rid of their apple mountain. If not, you can buy apples very cheaply. Introduce the children to the range of apples and their exotic names: Orange Pippins, Golden Delicious, James Grieve, Bramley, Russet, Spartan. Encourage the children to taste small pieces of each.

History

Apples have been grown in Britain at least since the Stone Age. We know this as dried apples have been found in the remains of Stone Age homes. Apples have featured in myths, legends, history and science. The Romans introduced many varieties of apples into Britain. There are many traditions and superstitions associated with apples - one custom is to carry cider to an orchard and to splash the roots of the most fruitful tree. A piece of bread is then dipped into the cider and hung on the branch of the tree. The revellers toast the tree, sing wassailing songs, blow horns, bang pans and drums.

WASSAILING

Wassailing is an ancient Christmas practice. The word comes from an old Anglo-Saxon toast 'Waes heil' which means 'be whole, be healthy'. A group of 'wassailers' went round with a bowl of hot ale to people's houses. They sang, offered drink and asked for more. In cider-making areas the apple orchards were toasted as in the following verse from a wassailing song.

Lily white Lily

Lily white lily, O lily white pin
Please to come down and let us come in
Lily white Lily, O lily white smock
Please to come down and pull back the lock.
   FOR IT'S OUR WASSAIL, JOLLY WASSAIL
   JOY COME TO OUR JOLLY WASSAIL
   SO WELL THEY MAY BLOOM, SO WELL THEY MAY BEAR
   THAT WE MAY HAVE APPLES AND CIDER NEXT YEAR.

Hedgerow Cookery and Seasonal Foods

APPLE SCONE ROUND
Makes 8 portions

200g (7oz) plain flour
½ teaspoon salt
2 teaspoons baking powder
50g (2oz) margarine
50g (2oz) sugar
2 peeled and grated apples
4 tablespoons milk

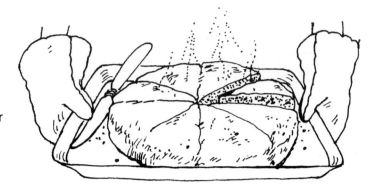

Sieve together the flour, salt and baking powder. Rub in the margarine. Add the sugar and the grated apple. Add enough milk to make a soft dough. Turn out onto a floured surface and knead lightly. Make the dough into a circle and put onto a greased baking tray. Score into eight pieces. Bake for twenty five minutes at 400°F/200°C (Gas Mark 4).

BAKED APPLES

Per person
1 apple
1 teaspoon honey
2 teaspoons dried fruit (sultanas, currants, apricots etc)
1 tablespoon water

Wash the apples and remove the cores. Make a cut in the skin around the middle of each apple. Place the apples in an ovenproof dish and fill the cavity of each apple with the honey, fruit and water. Bake for about 30 minutes at 350°F/180°C (Gas Mark 4).

APPLE AND NUT FRUIT SALAD

Combine a mixture of chopped fruit and nuts with a little lemon juice (to prevent the apple discolouring). Depending on what is available, the following could be used:

Apples, pears, bananas, oranges, grapes, kiwi fruit, apricots, peaches, nuts, chopped dates etc.

Art
Make a collage or print a frieze of an orchard. The trees may have cut-out leaf rubbings or leaf prints with the apples made from apple prints. For the bark use bark rubbings or corrugated paper. Make apple baskets from woven card. Paint children climbing trees and picking apples (see photograph on previous page).

Technology
Make apple recipe books (see photograph opposite). Involve the children in designing the books and making decisions about the size, the colour of the paper, the illustrations etc. Order cookery books from the library to use as reference books. Teach the children to use indexes. Point out the layout of the recipes and discuss why they are laid out in this way. After the children have selected the recipes, they can copy them by hand or put them on the word processor. Look at the design of books: the title page, dedication, contents, foreword, introduction etc. Ask them to think of a good title e.g. *A Glut of Apples* or *Apples Galore*. The construction of a book involves many curricular areas: maths, technology, design, craft, language and literacy skills.

Apple recipe book - see technical section on facing page

Further Activity
Suggest that the children make 'apple pigs' as follows:
One large apple
One small apple
Six cocktail sticks
Half a lemon (to rub on to the apple to stop it from going brown)

Put the big apple on its side and make legs out of the cocktail sticks. Attach half of the smaller apple to make the pig's head. Cut the snout from the other apple half. Attach with a cocktail stick. Make slits for the nostrils and add seeds. Use silver balls or seeds for the eyes.

Jars of homemade apply jelly and other preserves, decorated with labels and fabric pot-covers

Four and Twenty Blackbirds

PIES FOR THE RICH

- Read the nursery rhyme 'Sing a Song of Sixpence'. Explain that pies were sometimes made with live blackbirds. They were called 'surprise pies' and were produced to amuse the guests at banquets in the Middle Ages. The king or the lord of the manor would cut the crust and out would come birds or frogs. Sometimes even a child or a singing dwarf would emerge.
- As well as pies for fun, pies to eat were also common at the banquets. They were enormous and had fillings like swan, deer, pigeon, wild boar and porpoise.
- The food for banquets would take days to prepare and the menu makes the people appear very greedy. It might have looked like this.

Boar's head
Fish scented with rosemary
Sugared mackerel
Custard and marigolds
Stewed mutton
Roast kid
Venison pie
Spiced apples and figs

- Queen Elizabeth I paid a visit to a nobleman's house in 1561 and the servants spent days travelling around the countryside buying food. The shopping list included:

693 eggs
44 dishes of butter
7 gallons of cream
3 oxen
2 calves
6 sheep
a whole farmyard of poultry

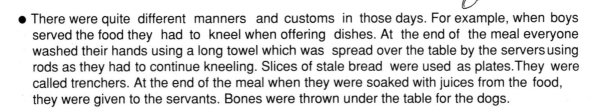

- There were quite different manners and customs in those days. For example, when boys served the food they had to kneel when offering dishes. At the end of the meal everyone washed their hands using a long towel which was spread over the table by the servers using rods as they had to continue kneeling. Slices of stale bread were used as plates. They were called trenchers. At the end of the meal when they were soaked with juices from the food, they were given to the servants. Bones were thrown under the table for the dogs.

Art and design
- Design your own surprise pies. What would you like to put into your pie to surprise people? Who is it for: your teacher, your mother, your friend? Draw and write about the scene when it is cut open.
- Class activity: make a large picture of a king with sponge- printed blackbirds flying out of a pie (see photograph opposite).
- Make surprise pies. Paint or make creatures of your choice e.g. butterflies, snakes, frogs, and attach them to sticks or straws. Push the stick into a 'pie crust' made with pastry, play dough or Plasticine (see photograph opposite).

Four and twenty blackbirds baked in a pie. When the pie was opened the birds began to sing

Sing a song of sixpence a pocket full of rye.

Wasn't that a dainty dish to set before the king?

look at what we put in our pies!

butterflies   snake   frogs   poppies

Writing
If you were giving a banquet for your friends, what would you have on your menu? You can be very greedy. Write an invitation to your banquet.

Drama / Role-Play
- Make a dance/mime/play using the nursery rhyme 'Sing a Song of Sixpence'. The children can be blackbirds, the king, queen, maid etc.
- Enact a medieval banquet observing manners and customs. What would the rich people at the table be talking about? What would the servants in the kitchen be talking about?

PIES FOR THE POOR
Traditionally pies have been a packed lunch dish for working people because they were easy to carry into the field, mines or factories. The pastry acted as a wrapper. Many parts of the country have their own special pies. Devon and Cornwall have pasties which they call 'oggies'. Scotland has meat and potato pies called 'bridies'. Glasgow has small mutton pies which used to be called 'tuppenny struggles' - perhaps because it was a struggle to find tuppence to pay for them. Cornish pasties sometimes had both a sweet and savoury filling in the same crust: half would be the main course and half the pudding. Now the filling is usually potato, turnip and meat but it used to vary depending on the customer's taste. Pork, rabbit, eggs, jam or fruit were all popular fillings. Initials in pastry were put on one end of the pasty to make sure someone didn't get a pasty with bacon filling if he had chosen mackerel. The initial end was eaten last in case it wasn't finished in one sitting. The traditional pasty had a very hard crust made from barley flour so that if it was dropped down a mineshaft, it would not break. Clotted cream was a luxury in poor families, but on rare occasions that some was available, they dolloped it on everything: pasties, pies, pilchards and potatoes. There is an abundance of mackerel off the coast of Devon now where once it was pilchards. Stargazy pie can be made with either.

Four and Twenty Blackbirds

Art / Design.
- If you could choose any filling for a Cornish pasty, what would you choose? Discuss fanciful possibilities. Draw a cross-section of your oggy.
- Make a collage picture of a Stargazy Pie (see photograph opposite).

Writing
- Write about how oggies, bridies, tuppenny struggles were named, and any other pies that you may have heard of.
- Write a recipe for a pie that you have invented. A pie can have almost any filling, so there is plenty of scope. Look at the correct layout for recipes and make your instructions clear. By studying other recipes estimate what would be suitable quantities. This can be done in pairs.

Recipes

HOMITY PIE
A satisfying and economical meal for 4 adults - plenty for the class to try

450g (1lb) potatoes, peeled and diced	2 crushed garlic cloves
450g (1lb) onions	1 tablespoon milk
25g (1oz) margarine	salt and pepper
100g (4oz) cheese - grated	300g (11oz) shortcrust pastry
Parsley (if available)	

Boil the potatoes until only just tender. Chop onions and sauté in margarine. Mix potatoes and onions. Add the cheese, garlic and milk (save some cheese for the top). Roll out the pastry and use it to line a flan dish. Add the potato and onion mixture. Sprinkle with the left-over cheese and parsley. Bake in oven at 400°F/200°C (Gas Mark 6) for 20 minutes.

TWO-IN-ONE OGGIES (PASTIES)
450g (1lb) of shortcrust pastry (makes about 8 saucer rounds or 4 large oggies)

Savoury half
A mixture of chopped up: potatoes, swedes, carrots, onions, peas
50g (2oz) minced meat (or grated cheese)
Salt, pepper, mixed herbs (1 teaspoon)

Sweet half
Peeled and diced cooking apple
Brown sugar
Roll out the pastry and cut into rounds (use saucers, small plates or dinner plates depending on what size pasties you want). Mix the savoury ingredients and place on one half of the pastry round and the sweet filling on the other. Dampen the pastry edge with milk. Draw the edges of each pasty together on the top of the filling and crimp the crust using finger and thumb. Put pastry initials on each end of the pasty (**M** for meat, **A** for apple). Put on a greased baking tray. Bake at 400°F/200°C (Gas Mark 6) for 15 minutes and then reduce to 325°F/160°C (Gas Mark 3) for another 30 minutes. Test the centre by pricking with a skewer or fork.

Silver foil fish displayed coming through sponge-printed pastry. Border of stars and ships

STARGAZY PIE
An extraordinary pie, fun to make and it looks dramatic

8 pilchards, sardines, herrings or small mackerel
2 chopped onions
parsley
salt and pepper
3 hard-boiled eggs
3 rashers streaky bacon
beaten egg to glaze
350g (12oz) shortcrust pastry

Clean and bone the fish, leaving on their heads. Stuff each fish with onion and parsley. Season. Halve the pastry and roll out each half. Use half to line a pie plate. Place the fish on the pastry, like spokes of a wheel, with their heads on the rim. Fill the gaps in between with chopped hard-boiled egg and bacon. Put the pastry lid in place. Press down between the fish heads to join the bottom pastry crust (wet the rims to make this easier). Brush with beaten egg. Bake for approximately 30 - 40 minutes at 400°F/200°C (Gas Mark 6) - the length of time depends on the size of the fish.

A Loaf of Bread, The Walrus said...

BREAD

History

Primitive people made bread from flour mixed with water. They made it into flat cakes and baked them over a fire. The ancient Egyptians were the first people to make leavened bread in about 2600 BC. It is said that a slave left some dough by the fire and fell asleep. When he awoke he was worried when he saw that the bread had grown to twice the size. Airborne yeast must have entered the dough. The Egyptians also invented a flour sieve to produce a finer flour. They were keen bread eaters and threw bread on the river Nile as a tribute to their gods. The builders of the pyramids were paid in loaves of bread. Bread was placed in the Egyptians' tombs as food to accompany the dead.

The Celts who lived in Britain in 500 BC baked bread in a pot with a lid which was buried in smouldering peat or cow dung. Because bread was a very important food for poor people, laws have been passed to control the size and price of loaves. Two hundred years ago, most people made their own bread. It was baked in brick ovens which had been heated by a fire. Compare the ancient methods of bread preparation with the very controlled conditions in modern bakeries.

Geography

Every country has developed its own bread specialities. Many of these are now available in other countries.

FRANCE - baguettes and croissants   SCANDINAVIA - crispbreads
ITALY - pizza and ciabatta (slipper)   GERMANY - pumpernickel
INDIA - chapati and naan bread   JEWISH - matzos (unleavened bread)
GREECE - pitta bread

Ask the children to name some other national breads. Also list the many varieties of English bread: muffins, crumpets, cottage loaves, Chelsea buns, milk loaves etc. Take as many as possible of these into the classroom. Arrange in baskets for the children to draw using pastels or coloured pencils. On a map of the world mark where the breads come from.

FLOUR

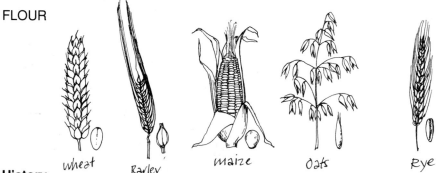

wheat   Barley   maize   Oats   Rye

History

Most bread in this country is made from wheat flour. Different kinds of bread use different parts of the wheat grain. Wholemeal bread is made from the whole grain. Wheat is made into flour by milling. Today the flour is milled in a factory using high speed machines. First the wheat is cleaned and dampened, then it is crushed by heavy rollers. It is shaken, crushed and sieved many times to make flour. Thousands of years ago people made flour by using two stones to crush dried grains of wheat. A saddlestone was a big stone shaped like a horse's saddle. It had a dip to sit in and another hollow were the grain would be ground. This method of making flour was very slow and tiring. Later a rotary-quern was used. Grain was poured into a hole in the centre and crushed between two stones. The top stone was turned by a handle. Windmills and watermills were common ways of milling until this century. Show the children different kinds of windmills and water mills. Discuss what would affect the location of these.

A Loaf of Bread, The Walrus said, is what we chiefly need

Windmill turning up in the air,
Tell us, what do you do up there?
If the wind comes blowing your way
Will you grind some corn today?

barley flour

wholemeal flour

strong plain flour

soya flour

rice flour

rye flour

A display of varieties of bread (including this wheatsheaf) in front of harvest picture with border of cut-out flour bags and raffia wheatsheaves

CHEESE SCONES
Makes 12 scones

225g (8oz) plain flour
½ level teaspoon salt
2½ level teaspoons baking powder
50g (2oz) butter of margarine
100g (4oz) grated cheese
About 150ml (¼ pt) milk

Mix together the flour, salt and baking powder. Rub in the butter until it resembles fine breadcrumbs. Stir in the cheese and gradually add the milk, mixing it until the dough is soft and manageable. Knead the dough lightly on a floured surface. Roll out to about 3cm thickness and cut into 12 equal portions. (You may sprinkle more grated cheese on top.) Bake the scones for 12 to 15 minutes at 425°F/220°C (Gas Mark 7).

A Loaf of Bread, The Walrus said, is what we chiefly need

MAKE YOUR OWN FLOUR

Materials needed: Some grains of wheat (available from a farmer, a mill, a seed merchant or a pet shop), some flat stones and flour sieve.
Take the grains of wheat from the ear. Grind the grains between the stones (best done in pairs in order to take turns, as it is hard work). When there is enough flour, sieve it. Look at the flour and the contents of the sieve. Feel the flour. Compare it with different types of shop-bought flour: strong white, self-raising, plain white, wholemeal, granary.

TESTING FLOUR FOR STRENGTH

Some flour is 'stronger' than others. You can test the strength of flour in this way:-
Weigh 100g (4oz) flour. Add 50ml (2fl oz) of water to make a ball of dough. Do this with each type of flour. Make the dough balls into circles with a diameter of 10cms. Put each circle of dough on to a piece of graph paper and then on to a board. Put another board with a 2kg weight on top. After five minutes measure the new diameter. The stronger the flour, the less the diameter of the circle will have increased. Design a suitable table for recording the results. Ask the children to list other foods that are made from flour (pies, cakes, biscuits, pancakes, sauces, buns, croissants).

YEAST

To make bread rise and become less stodgy, yeast is added. Yeast is a microscopic organism. When yeast and sugar are added to dough *fermentation* takes place. It produces a gas called carbon dioxide which fills the dough with bubbles and makes it rise. At this stage the yeast is alive but it is killed in the hot oven. Yeast can be bought fresh or dried. Look at both. Feel them and smell them. Which can you keep the longest? Name some more dried foods.

Science

This experiment shows the best conditions for yeast to ferment. Take two test tubes. In each put 1g of sugar, 2g fresh yeast and 10ml of water - warm water in one, cold water in the other. Put a balloon over the end of each test tube. Put the test tube with warm water in a warm place and the other in a cold place. Record what happens to each balloon at fifteen minute intervals. What is the clearest way of displaying the findings?

INDIAN BREADS

There are many different kinds of bread in India and one kind or another is eaten with every meal in Northern India. The flour used in India is *ata* which is available in Indian grocers. Many of the breads are fried, not baked like British breads.
POORIS - These are very puffy.
PARATHAS - These are triangular breads that are sometimes taken to school for lunch.
NAAN - This bread is baked in very hot clay ovens called *tandooris*. It is stuck to the sides of the oven.
CHAPATIS - Sometimes chapatis are small and thin and sometimes large and thick.

A Loaf of Bread, The Walrus said, is what we chiefly need

Bread models (see recipe instructions on page 22)

CHAPATI
250g (9oz) wholewheat flour
175ml (6fl oz) water
Vegetable oil

Put flour in a bowl. Slowly add water and mix into a soft dough. Knead for three to five minutes. Cover with a damp cloth and leave to rest for half an hour. Knead again for a few minutes and divide into twelve pieces. Flatten the pieces with a rolling pin and cover them with flour. Pat the chapati between your hands. Put into an oiled frying pan. (In India a *tava* is used, which is a slightly concave iron plate.) Fry gently for a minute on each side. In India it would be put on hot charcoal to make it puff up. They may be eaten straight from the pan spread with butter.

IRISH SODA BREAD
Makes 8 portions

450g (1lb) plain flour	25g (1oz) margarine
2 level teaspoons	300ml (½ pt) soured milk OR
bicarbonate of soda	dried skimmed milk and water
2 level teaspoons	1 level teaspoon salt
cream of tartar	(N.B.⅔ wholemeal:⅓ plain flour may be used)

Sift the flour, bicarbonate of soda, cream of tartar and salt into a bowl. Cut up the margarine and rub it into the flour with the fingertips until the mixture resembles fine breadcrumbs. Make a well in the centre of the flour mixture, add the milk (soured with 1 tablespoon of lemon juice) or the skimmed milk mixture, and mix to a soft, manageable dough, working the ingredients with a round-bladed knife. Turn the dough onto a floured board, knead lightly and shape into an 18cm (7 inch) round; flatten it slightly. Mark the round into four with a knife, set it on a floured baking tray and bake in the centre of the oven at 400°F/200°C (Gas Mark 6) for about 30 minutes. Cool slightly and serve warm. This bread does not keep well and is best enjoyed on the day it is made.

A Loaf of Bread, The Walrus said, is what we chiefly need

CHALLA
Challa is a plaited white loaf that Jewish families eat on their Sabbath day (Shabbat), which is Saturday. Traditionally, dark bread would be eaten throughout the week and the white challa loaf baked specially for Shabbat. The Shabbat is a time of rest and renewal so the bread would be made in advance. The Friday evening meal (which is the start of Shabbat) begins with the ritual washing of hands and then the breaking of bread. Bread is broken rather than cut because it is considered that knives should not be on the table on a day of peace. Two loaves are always on the table for the Friday night meal.

Recipe
15g (½ oz) fresh yeast
225ml (8fl oz) warm water
1 tablespoon of caster sugar
25g (1oz) melted margarine
1 teaspoon salt
1 egg
450g (1lb) strong white flour

For glaze:
1 beaten egg
poppy seeds

Mix the yeast with half warm water and sugar. Leave until it starts to froth. Add the margarine, salt and beaten egg. Add the flour gradually. Add the rest of the liquid. Knead for a few minutes and leave to prove for one hour. Make the dough into two plaited loaves. Brush with beaten egg and sprinkle with poppy seeds. Put on a greased tray and bake in a preheated oven 425°F/220°C (Gas Mark 7) for 35 mins.

Questions
What day is the Jewish Sabbath?
What day is the Christian Sabbath?

Discussion
Should shops be open on Sunday?
Encourage children to see all sides of the argument. After a class discussion they could take an opinion poll amongst their parents, teachers, other children.

GARLIC BREAD
100g (4oz) softened butter
1 clove garlic (crushed)

1 tablespoon parsley
1 loaf French bread

Cream the butter with the garlic and parsley. Cut the bread into fairly thick slices crosswise but not completely through to the bottom of the loaf. Spread the butter mixture on one side of each slice and wrap in foil. Place on a baking tray and bake for 15 - 20 minutes at 400°F/200°C (Gas Mark 6). Serve hot.

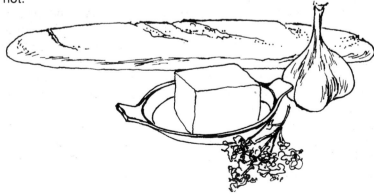

A Loaf of Bread, The Walrus said, is what we chiefly need

CRUNCHY OAT BREAD

250g (9oz) wholemeal flour
1 teaspoon baking powder
½ teaspoon bicarbonate of soda
½ teaspoon salt
25g (1oz) butter
75g (3oz) rolled oats

25g (1oz) wheatgerm
125ml (4fl oz) sour cream
2 eggs (lightly beaten)
75g (3oz) soft brown sugar
Variations: Add 1 teaspoon mixed spice
or 50g (2oz) sultanas or walnuts

Sift the flour, baking powder, bicarbonate of soda and salt into a large bowl and rub in the butter. Add the oats and wheatgerm and mix. In another bowl, mix the sour cream, eggs and sugar and beat the mixture well. Make a well in the centre of the flour mixture and pour in the cream mixture. Mix until it is a soft dough. Put into a greased 1lb loaf tin and bake at 350°F/180°C (Gas Mark 4) for 40 - 45 minutes. Cool on a wire rack.

FRUIT AND MALT BREAD

200ml (7 fl oz) warm water
25g (1oz) soft margarine
2 tablespoons malt extract
1 tablespoon black treacle
25g (1oz) fresh yeast **OR** 1 teaspoon dried yeast (mixed with 1 teaspoon sugar)

225g (8oz) wholewheat flour
225g (8oz) plain flour
150g (5oz) sultanas
sugar and water to glaze

Pour the liquid into a bowl and add margarine in small pieces, malt extract, treacle and yeast. Mix thoroughly. Add flour and sultanas and mix well. Knead until the dough is smooth and elastic. Shape into two small loaves. This dough is quite soft. Place the loaves onto a greased baking sheet, cover and prove until they have doubled in size. Bake at 400°F/200°C (Gas Mark 6) for 40-45 minutes. Cool on wire rack and then brush with glaze made from sugar and water.

Bread dough is very versatile and it is easy to add ingredients or change the shape to make a totally different type of food, for example, add chopped nuts, dried vine fruits, dates, dried figs, apricots, glacé fruits, mashed bananas, spices to make a fruit and nut bread of your choice. Add savoury ingredients like chopped onions, cheese, herbs and savoury spices. Add seeds to the tops of your bread rolls, for example, poppy, sesame, mustard, caraway seeds as well as rough-milled grains and wholegrains. You can make the dough into a flat pizza shape and top it with tomatoes, cheese, olives and any other ingredients that you would like on a pizza. Rolls can be plaited, knotted, whorled, patterned with cuts; decorated with dough leaves and flowers; glazed with beaten egg. The dough can be baked in loaf tins, fluted tins, terracotta flower pots. It can be rolled out into sticks about an inch wide to make bread sticks which can also be twisted or plaited; dough can be made into balls the size of a golf ball for tiny rolls. Encourage the children to make their own variations in taste and shape.

A Loaf of Bread, The Walrus said, is what we chiefly need

MODELLING IN BREAD

Bread is a good modelling medium and the results make welcome presents for all occasions. The following recipe is quick and easy.

QUICK BREAD
(You can use fresh yeast to demonstrate its live quality)

1½ kg (3¼ lb) wholemeal flour
50g (2oz) margarine
1 teaspoon salt
30g (1¼ oz) yeast
1 teaspoon brown sugar
Warm water

Rub margarine into flour and add salt. Mix yeast with sugar, stir until runny and add a cup of warm water. Make a well in the middle of flour and pour in yeast mixture. Cover with a sprinkling of flour and leave until bubbly. Add warm water gradually, kneading together until the dough feels stretchy: not too wet and not too dry. (It should feel like a cushion.) Knead thoroughly. Leave it to rise until double the size. Knead again. (This bread can be made with half wholemeal and half white flour.)
Give the children a selection of seeds (pumpkin, sunflower, sesame, poppy), and raisins and nuts. They can now begin modelling - teddy bears, hedgehogs, mice, crocodiles, plaits and wreaths are all possibilities (see photograph on page l9).

Play Area
Make a 'baker's shop' in the play area. Provide tray, baskets, labels, paper bags, coins and a baker's apron. This could be a short term activity with edible bread, or a longer term activity if the bread products were hard-baked and preserved with PVA or varnish.

Vocabulary
Aerate, air pocket, bubble, volume, edible, inedible, fermentation, microscopic, leavened, baker's dozen.

Maths
If possible, visit the local baker's shop. Find out prices of bread, and label the loaves in your play area for simple money practice.

Songs: 'Pat-a-cake, pat-a-cake, baker's man'; 'Five currant buns in a baker's shop'.

Eco-Cooking

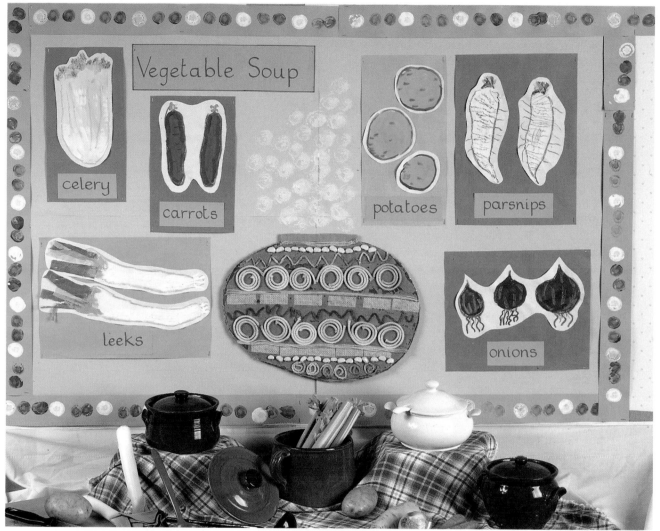

See recipe on Page 25

Vegetarians believe that eating meat is not only unhealthy but is an economically unsound way of using the world's resources. For example, Britain imports large quantities of grain to feed animals which become food for us. It takes a great deal of grain to produce a small amount of meat, and a vegetarian diet would be far cheaper to sustain.

Discussion

CONSERVATION
- Water is vital for all life - don't waste or pollute it. Ask the children to suggest ways of saving water and keeping our supplies unpolluted. Examples: don't leave the tap running when washing hands or teeth; use uncoloured, unbleached, recycled toilet paper; have a shallow bath or a shorter shower; use washing-up water to water plants.
- Air - How can we keep our air clean? Examples: use the car less; use smokeless fuel; use lead- free petrol.
- Energy - Oil, gas, coal produce energy. They will not last forever - so we need to *conserve* energy. How can we do this at home? at school? Examples: plan cooking so that the oven is not half-empty; use a pressure cooker or hay box; steam one vegetable whilst boiling another; switch off lights, televisions, etc. when you leave a room.

Eco-Cooking

PACKAGING

Look at the food wrappings in a bag of shopping. Which of it is essential for hygiene? Which of it is unnecessary? Which wrappings are there to advertise the product? We pay extra for all this packing and its disposal. Consider the following food packages that use valuable resources.

- Cans use up fuel and metal. Many are difficult to recycle because they are made from a combination of metals which are difficult to separate.
- Paper and cardboard use trees. It takes a forest the size of Wales to provide enough trees for Britain for one year.
- Plastics are made from oil. The plastics don't rot - so they pollute the environment forever. What can we do?

Small group work: make a list of ways to minimise wrappings.

Art and Design

Make posters to display in the school to remind everyone to look after our environment. Think of an eye-catching design and message. Decide where the best places would be to put them.

Activities

Collect all the wrappings from everyone's packed lunch. Weigh them. Sort them into biodegradable and non-biodegradable material. Make them into a huge collage. It could be a person or a big tree or an abstract picture. (See photograph opposite.)

Vocabulary

Biodegradeable, decompose, preservation, conservation, wasteful, economy.

MAKE A HAY-BOX

Traditionally, a hay-box was just that: a box with a lid, filled with hay. If you do not have a ready supply of hay, the same effect can be achieved by using a strong cardboard box filled with tightly crumpled newspaper. Explain about heat retention and insulation. The following dishes can be cooked in a hay-box. Bring the ingredients to the boil on the cooker and then transfer to the hay-box. Baked beans or vegetable soup may be cooked effectively in a hay-box.

HARICOT BAKED BEANS - American Style

450g (1lb) dried haricot beans
Water
¾ teaspoon dry mustard
pinch of ginger
2 tablespoons sugar
3 tablespoons black treacle
50g (2oz) margarine
1 tin of tomatoes

Soak beans overnight, drain and wash. Bring to the boil in enough water to cover and boil for 5 minutes. Put into hay-box and test after 2-3 hours. Drain when cooked. Add a fresh 300 ml (½ pt) of water and the remaining ingredients. Bring back to the boil and put back into hay-box for a further hour.
The same recipe could be boiled for 5 minutes then cooked in the oven at 350°F/180°C (Gas Mark 4) for one hour and then just re-heated after the remaining ingredients are added.

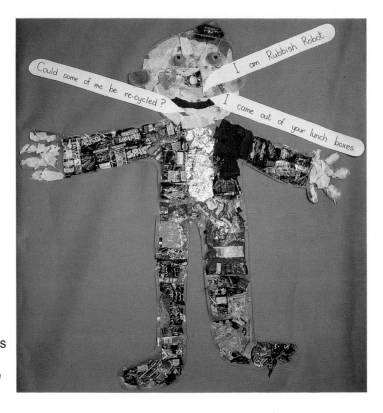

Could some of me be re-cycled?

I am Rubbish Robot.

I came out of your lunch boxes.

**Collage made from lunch box wrappings
(see Activities on facing page)**

Recipes

VEGETABLE SOUP
Approx 8 - 10 bowls or enough for
the class to taste

1 onion	2 carrots
1 large potato	25g (1oz) butter
4 sticks celery	1 litre (1¾ pts) water
2 leeks	1 can chopped tomatoes
2 parsnips	- optional
	fresh herbs, if available
	salt and pepper

Wash and slice the vegetables. Heat the butter. Sauté the onion in the butter and then add other vegetables. Fry for about 5 minutes. Add the liquids and the seasoning. Simmer for half an hour **OR** bring the mixture to the boil on the cooker and then place in the hay-box. It should cook in about 3 hours: a lot depends on how well insulated the box is.

STUFFED MARROW
Every year there seems to be a glut of marrows. Before cooking a marrow, it can be weighed, measured, painted and admired.
Makes plenty for a class to taste

1 large marrow	50g (2oz) cheddar cheese - grated
1 large onion - sliced	225g (8oz) cottage cheese
100g (4oz) mushrooms - sliced	mixed dried herbs
100g (4oz) tomatoes - chopped	25g (1oz) butter

Cut the marrow in half lengthwise. Scoop out the seeds to hollow the insides. Sprinkle the flesh with salt, and leave the two halves upside down on kitchen paper to drain. Mix together all the ingredients for the filling. Wipe the inside of the marrow, dry and fill with the stuffing. Put the two halves together and wrap securely in foil. Bake for about an hour in the oven at 350°F/ 180°C (Gas Mark 4) **OR** place in the hay-box for about 3 hours.

Maths
ECO - nomics
● Compare the cost of a commercially produced can of baked beans with the equivalent amount of home-made baked beans. Perhaps you could taste both and make a graph showing the preferences.
● Repeat both of the above activities with vegetable soup.

Highdays and Holidays

CHRISTMAS

ADVENT

Advent can be the start of Christmas activities. If it does not coincide with a Monday, the first Monday in December could be treated as Advent Day and the whole day devoted to making Christmas decorations, with each teacher planning three or four decorations that will be made in his/her classroom. As many parents as possible could be encouraged to help; possibly some will also arrive with more ideas. The children then choose in which area they want to work.

CHRISTMAS DECORATIONS

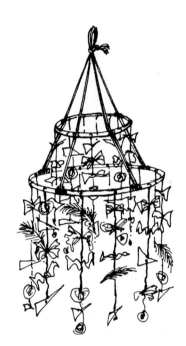

- **Christmas mobile**
  This unusual mobile works well as a group activity.
  Materials: Strong florists' wire, squares (about 10cms)
  of foil, tissue paper, crêpe paper,
  white feathers, white wool, darning needles, ribbon.

Make two wire circles with diameters of 30cm and 80cm approx. Cut the wool into one metre lengths. Thread darning needles with wool. Thread pieces of tissue, foil and crêpe paper on to the wool leaving short spaces in between each one. Twist them around the thread to stop them slipping. Tie white feathers at intervals. Then hang the smaller circle just above the large circle and attach ribbons to the top circle for hanging. When there are sufficient streamers, knot each length to the two rings. These streamers also look good on the Christmas tree instead of tinsel. A limited range of colours looks best: red, white and silver; or blue, green, white and silver.

- **Swags**
  Take a long length of rope. Collect lots of greenery.
  Make into small bunches and attach to the rope with wire.
  Intersperse with wired fir cones and ribbon bows.
  Loop the swags along the corridors.

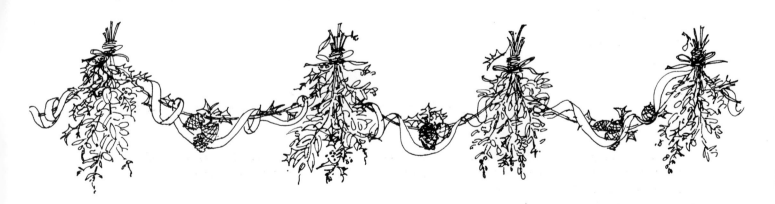

Hand-printed tree, dough figures and dough wreaths (see instructions below)

● **A tree from hand prints**

Each child makes several hand prints in paint. Green is the obvious choice, but shades of blue and purple look effective. When dry, the prints are cut out leaving some white round the fingers. Glue or staple them to the wall in a large triangle with all the fingers pointing downwards and each row of hands overlapping. Decorate with dough decorations. (See photograph above.)

● **Dough decorations**

These can be adapted to all age ranges.

Recipe

Two cups of self-raising flour to two cups of salt and approximately one cup of water. Mix well and knead.

– Christmas decorations. Roll out the dough and use pastry cutters to make the wreaths and shapes. Bake in slow oven for two hours. Leave plain or paint red or green. Glue on sequins. (See photograph above.)
– Plain red hearts can look very effective.
– Dough figures: snowmen, trees, angels, choirboys, birds etc. to make a Christmas scene on cotton wool. Bake and paint as above. (See photograph.)

All these will need varnishing.

Highdays and Holidays

Advent Day could end with an assembly where the meaning of Advent is discussed, and Advent biscuits made by the children are eaten.

ADVENT BISCUITS
Makes approximately 30 biscuits

350g (12oz) flour
l teaspoon cinnamon
2 teaspoons ginger
2 teaspoons grated lemon rind
l00g (4oz) butter
7 teaspoons honey (runny)
Juice of 1 lemon

Mix dry ingredients and lemon rind. Rub in butter. Melt honey and add to mixture. Add lemon juice and sufficient water to form a firm dough. Knead lightly. Roll and cut out shapes. Put on a greased baking tray and bake for 20 minutes 350˚F/l80˚C (Gas Mark 4). Ice and decorate if required.

CHRISTMAS ORGANISATION

Have a Christmas art table full of special materials: glitter, silver and gold pens, coloured foil, feathers, old wrapping paper and cards, cotton wool, tissue paper etc. Buy small calendars to make into gifts. Allow the children some freedom to design and make their own calendars, cards, decorations, but encourage careful plans and designs first.

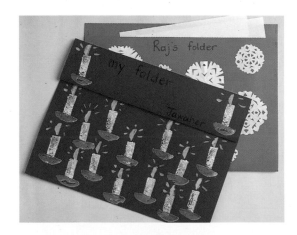

See instructions below

CHRISTMAS FOLDERS
After Advent Day each child could make a Christmas folder in which is stored all the work produced until the end of term. The folder can be decorated in a variety of ways:
- with simple leaf prints (yellow and orange on black looks good)
- with potato prints of candles (see photograph above)
- with snowflakes made in the usual way from folding and snipping, then glued on to the folder
  (see photograph above)
- or let the children decorate the folders as they wish.

CHRISTMAS CARDS
A book could be devoted to this topic alone so just one suggestion: professionally printed cards from the children's own drawings and prints sell well and can make money to finance the class's Christmas cooking. Lino cuts and polystyrene prints particularly make effective cards.

CHRISTMAS FOOD

Collage Christmas pudding made from coloured magazine cuttings; ingredients drawn on paper plates and labelled

THE GEOGRAPHY OF THE CHRISTMAS PUDDING
● Ask the children to copy a recipe for Christmas pudding and decorate this for their folders.
● Collect the ingredients in a basket and find out where they all came from. Attach strings from the different ingredients to the place of their origin on a world map.

Mini puddings can be made using small tin foil cases or heatproof plastic bowls (see photograph)

Art
Make a collage Christmas pudding from cut or torn coloured paper and display with paper plates showing the pudding ingredients (see main photograph above).

Highdays and Holidays

CHRISTMAS CAKES

**Miniature Christmas cakes -
use any traditional recipe**

Candle cakes (see recipe below)

The same activities as for Christmas pudding on the previous page can be carried out with Christmas cakes. Small 8oz baked bean tins or sweetcorn tins make good baking containers for individual cakes. Decorated attractively, these are useful presents for grandparents or parents (see photograph). Use a traditional Christmas cake recipe, or make candle cakes as follows:

CANDLE CAKES

75g (3oz) butter or hard margarine	50g (2oz) ground almonds
50g (2oz) vegetable fat	2 large eggs, beaten
150g (5oz) caster sugar	150g (5oz) plain flour
2 drops almond essence	

Cream butter, fat, sugar and almond essence. Beat in ground almonds. Add eggs a little at a time, beating well. Fold in flour. Grease and line 4 x 425gm soup tins. Half fill with mixture. Cook at 350°F/180°C (Gas Mark 4) for 45 minutes.

HOMEMADE SWEETS
 None of these recipes need cooking

FONDANT
This basic recipe can be used for a variety of sweets by adding different colourings and flavourings - makes about 40

1 egg white
450g (1lb) icing sugar
pinch of cream of tartar
2 teaspoons water
l teaspoon lemon juice
Whip egg white until stiff. Mix all ingredients. Knead for 5 minutes. Leave for an hour or chill for 30 minutes.
- Add a few drops of peppermint essence and green colouring for peppermint creams, or
- Add coconut and pink colouring, or
- Add chopped glacé cherries.

These sweets can be cut into star, heart, circle or flower shapes. The mixture can also be used for sugar mice using silver balls for eyes and fine string for tails.

l. Cereal boxes, painted and decorated, for carrying home Christmas presents (see page 32).

2. Christingle oranges, which are carried by children at the Christingle Service - the orange representing the world, the candle signifying Jesus Christ as the light of the world, and the four sticks with their sweets or raisins symbolising the four corners of the earth, and its fruits. The service originated in Czechoslovakia - and is a simple and effective service for parents to attend - the symbols of the orange are explained, and hymns sung.

SESAME SEED SWEETS
l2 tablespoons sesame seeds (toasted dry in a frying pan)
4 tablespoons honey
a little flour to mix
rice paper
Mix seeds and honey and add flour to stiffen. Press thinly onto rice paper on a baking tray. Leave to harden in fridge. Cut into squares.

TRUFFLES
Makes approx 30 truffles

100g (4oz) butter
l00g (4oz) sugar
Rum essence
Almond essence
4 teaspoons cocoa powder
l50g (5oz) ground almonds
l00g (4oz) cake crumbs
extra cocoa/drinking chocolate or chocolate vermicelli to roll the truffles in

Cream butter and sugar. Add few drops of rum essence, almond essence and cocoa. Beat, then add almonds and cake crumbs. Roll into little balls the size of walnuts and dip in chocolate vermicelli or cocoa powder.

STUFFED DATES
Stone dates, and replace each stone with half a walnut.

Highdays and Holidays

Art
CHRISTMAS PRESENT CONTAINERS
For best results, turn cereal packets inside out and reseal with masking tape. Cut hole in one side, then paint and decorate with tissue paper rosettes. (See photograph on previous page.)

WRAPPINGS FOR SWEETS
● Découpage boxes - cover small boxes with cut-out scraps from old wrapping paper, then varnish.
● Paint patterns on jam jars (silver and gold paint look festive) and add red felt frilly tops.
● Make cones from shiny paper, and add doily lining. Cut three dinner plate sized circles in tissue or Cellophane (different colours). Fill with sweets and tie with ribbon.

MINCE PIES

History
● Mince pies were popular Christmas fare from Elizabethan times. They were called shred or minced pies after the spiced, minced meat filling. The meat was mixed with suet, dried fruit, orange and lemon peel and sugar.
● In the 1700s it was discovered that this filling would keep for a long time if mixed with brandy and if the meat was added at the last minute. Later, people started to miss out the meat altogether and mince pies were made as we know them today without the minced meat.

Recipe
Makes approximately 30 pies

100g (4oz) suet	100g (4oz) sugar
100g (4oz) currants	Juice and rind of one lemon
100g (4oz) raisins	25g (1oz) sultanas
1 small finely chopped apple	I teaspoon brandy (optional)

pinch each of nutmeg, mace and cinnamon
N.B. Suet is now available made from vegetable oils; this is a healthier alternative to suet made from saturated animal fat.

Mix all the ingredients together thoroughly for filling.

For pastry
450g (1lb) plain flour
225g (8oz) margarine
pinch salt
4-6 tbs water
Rub flour and margarine together until mixture looks like breadcrumbs. Add salt and water to bind the pastry. Roll out evenly and use small cutters to make individual mince pies.(You could perhaps try making Elizabethan mince pies by adding, say, 450g (1lb) of cooked mince meat to this recipe.) Bake for 20 minutes at 350°F/180°C (Gas Mark 4).

Valentine Tree collage with heart tarts

VALENTINE'S DAY

A feast was held in ancient Rome during February called Lupercalia. The names of young men and women were put into a box, shaken and then picked out. It is thought that the Bishop Valentine of Rome was martyred on the eve of this feast in the third century and so the day acquired his name. Birds are supposed to choose a mate on this day too.

Art and Craft

A VALENTINE TREE

Make a large tree either by painting or by collage (corrugated paper works well) and decorate the branches with paper leaves and tissue blossom. Cut out heart shapes and let the children write a 'Valentine message' about someone in the class e.g.'I like Mary because she lets me share her crisps,' 'I like John's blonde hair' etc. Some engineering is required so that each person has a Valentine heart written about them. One way is to write everyone's name on paper and for each child to take a name. (See photograph above.)

Language

● Make Valentine's greetings by finding a suitable adjective for each letter of the alphabet e.g.
   You are **A**dorable, **B**eautiful, **C**lever, **D**elightful, etc.
● Invent a code to write a Valentine message. Give the children some possible examples
   e.g. J MPWF ZPV or H KNUD XNT - How do these codes work?

VALENTINE TEA

Using a heart-shaped cutter, cut out bread hearts from sliced bread. Spread thinly with strawberry jam, and make into sandwiches. Serve with heart-decorated jam tarts. (See photograph above.)

QUEEN OF HEARTS' TARTS

Make jam tarts and decorate the tops with pastry hearts - approx 15 tarts
225g (8oz) flour
100g (4oz) margarine
raspberry jam
water
Make shortcrust pastry by rubbing margarine into the flour until it resembles breadcrumbs. Add water gradually to bind mixture. Roll out to approximately 5mm thickness. Cut into small rounds and place in a greased patty tin. Add a teaspoon of jam to each round. Cut out small hearts and place on top of the jam tarts. Bake for 20 minutes at 400°F/200°C (Gas Mark 6).

Highdays and Holidays

SHROVE TUESDAY

The Tuesday, which is 41 days before Easter, is Shrove Tuesday. It is the eve of the first day of Lent. Lent is supposed to be a time of quietness and fasting for forty days, so Shrove Tuesday was a day when people had lots of fun and food. It used to be called Mischief Day. It was the last time people could eat 'luxury' foods before Lent, so traditional Shrove Tuesday dishes used up the remains of left-over foods that would be forbidden in Lent. The most usual food to be made was pancakes which is why Shrove Tuesday was given the nickname Pancake Tuesday. Other dishes were made in different parts of Britain: broth in Scotland, doughnuts in Hertfordshire, pea soup in Cornwall, frying-pan pudding in Lincolnshire. In the past, people were too poor for pancakes and so they used to go begging for the ingredients. It was called 'shroving' and they chanted as they went:
'Lard's scarce and flour's dear,
That's what makes me come shroving here.'

Besides having fun and mischief on Shrove Tuesday, traditionally people went to have their sins forgiven or 'shriven' before Lent began.

TRADITIONAL GAMES FOR SHROVE TUESDAY
FREE FOR ALL FOOTBALL
This game is one which whole villages played for fun on Shrove Tuesday. It is football without any rules and fun to play in school on this day. The teams can have any number of players and the goal posts can be fixed anywhere. (Sometimes they were put at either end of the village.) The ball can be kicked, carried or thrown.
PANCAKE TOSSING RELAY RACE
Make two teams. Each has a frying-pan and a pancake. The first child runs to a certain spot and returns, tossing the pancake as he/she runs. The pan is then passed to the next child in the team and so on until each child has completed the race. The winning team is the one that finishes first.

Recipes
PEA SOUP
Makes 6 large bowls, or plenty for the class to taste

25g (1oz) butter	l litre (1¾ pts) water mixed with (optional)
2 choppped onions	chicken or vegetable stock
scraps of bacon or ham	450g (1lb) dried peas left to soak in cold water overnight
pepper and salt	teaspoon dried or fresh herbs

Melt the butter in a large pan. Gently fry the onion and bacon (or ham). Add the water. Drain the peas and add to the pan. Add pepper, salt and herbs. Simmer for 1½ hours until the peas are mushy. Season to taste.

PANCAKES

250g (9oz) plain flour	450ml (¾ pt) milk
pinch of salt	25g (1oz) butter
2 eggs	

Sieve the flour into a large bowl. Add the eggs and salt. Mix together. Slowly add the milk, whisking continually. Melt a tiny piece of the butter in a frying-pan. Pour in enough mixture to thinly cover the bottom of the pan. When the mixture looks dry, shake the pancake, toss it in the air, catch it in the pan and cook the other side. Repeat until all the batter is used.

A painting of the custom of throwing coloured water, from the story of Krishna

HOLI - THE HINDU FESTIVAL OF SPRING

Myths, legends and customs associated with Holi vary from region to region of India. Most, however, involve lighting a bonfire, throwing coloured water or paints over each other and eating festive food together. Hindu stories are re-told or acted in many parts of India. The story of Prahlad explains why bonfires are lit.

THE STORY OF PRAHLAD - Prahlad believed in God. His father did not. He wanted Prahlad to treat him as God, but Prahlad refused. His father tried to kill him. He ordered his soldiers to throw Prahlad into a pit of snakes. Prahlad was bitten by many snakes but he did not die, as God saved him. The king then sent a herd of elephants to trample over his son while he slept. God protected Prahlad again. Finally, the king asked his wicked sister Holika to help him. Fire could not harm Holika so she led Prahlad into a fire believing that he would die and she be would be safe, but God led Prahlad out of the fire unharmed and Holika was burned to death.

Tell the story of Prahlad. It can be re-told using mime or dance. Zig-zag frieze books can be made to tell the story with pictures and writing.

Throwing coloured water is associated with Krishna's wooing of a beautiful young girl called Radha. Playfully, he threw some coloured water at her. In school, coloured paper could be thrown to have fun but avoid the mess.

The following would be a good drink to have around the bonfire for the celebration of Holi.

MASALA CHAI (Spiced tea)

600ml (1pt) water	175ml (6fl oz) milk
2.5cm (1 inch) stick of cinnamon	6 teaspoons sugar
8 cardamom pods	3 teaspoons loose black tea leaves
8 whole cloves	

Put the water in a saucepan and add the cinnamon, cardamom and cloves. Bring to the boil. Cover and turn heat to low. Simmer for 10 minutes. Add the milk and sugar. Bring to a simmer again. Add the tea leaves and turn off the heat. After 2 minutes, strain the tea and serve immediately.

Highdays and Holidays

PASSOVER/PESACH - A JEWISH FESTIVAL OF THANKSGIVING

This festival is to commemorate the time when the Jews left Egypt where they had been slaves under the Pharoahs. They give thanks to God for their freedom. During Pesach, human rights, political freedom, racism and totalitarianism are given much thought.

Pesach falls around the same time as Easter in the Christian calendar. It lasts a week and during that time the food eaten in a Jewish household is symbolic of the origin of the Holy Days. In their hurry to escape from Egypt and their life as slaves, the Israelites did not wait for the dough to rise. Instead they baked flat loaves - matzah (unleavened bread). During Pesach no food that involves fermentation (hametz) is eaten. This means no leavened bread, no cakes, no beer, no biscuits, no pasta, no yeast extract, no whisky. Everything that is made with flour is given away to non-Jews or eaten up the night before Passover. The last bits are burnt or thrown to the wind. From then on only Passover food is eaten. This is done to show that release from slavery is total and involves all levels of existence.

Passover suppers - *sedarim* - are usually large gatherings. The leader of the *seder* says: 'Let all who are hungry come and eat. Let all who are in need come and celebrate the Passover.'

If there are any Jewish people in your neighbourhood, ask if they would be willing to come and tell the children about the Passover.

Recipes

CINNAMON BALLS
Makes approximately 20
2 egg whites
175g (6oz) ground almonds
75g (3oz) caster sugar
1 tablespoon cinnamon
icing sugar

Whisk the egg whites until stiff. Add the ground almonds, sugar and cinnamon. Roll into small balls. Bake on a greased tray at 350°F/l80°C (Gas Mark 4) for 25 minutes. They should be slightly soft inside. Cool for 5 minutes, then roll in icing sugar.

CHAROSET
Charoset is a traditional Passover dish. It is a mixture of fruit and nuts ground together to form a paste. This symbolises the 'mortar' used by the Israelites building cities in Egypt. There are many versions of this dish. The Israelis use bananas, dates and peanuts while in the Yemen the dish has spices and figs. The following are common ingredients, but it is possible to adapt according to taste.

2 large apples
75g (3oz) almonds, blanched and skinned

2 teaspoons cinnamon
2 tablespoons Kosher wine (or grape or apple juice)

Chop the apples and almonds very finely. This can be done in a food processor, or they can be grated. Sprinkle with the cinnamon. Mix to a paste with the wine or juice.

Vocabulary
Pharoah, slavery, oppression, oppressor, liberty, independence, fermentation, thanksgiving, gratitude, deliverance.

School Cafés

Menu, poster and invitation for a class tearoom

Most schools engage in non-stop fund-raising, whether it is for charity or for school equipment. Sponsored activities are popular, but a very enjoyable alternative to these can be school cafés. These cafés can take place at the end of the school day and be organised on a class basis.

PLANNING

This should be done with the children. Careful planning is essential to guarantee the smooth running of the event, and also to engage and enthuse the children.

- Decide with the class which is the best afternoon for a café, avoiding days, if possible, when a number of the children are having to leave on time for swimming or other activities.
- Choose a venue. It can be the classroom, school hall, or outdoors in summer. Decide how it is to be decorated. This may depend on whether the café is going to have a theme (see below).
- Make a list of equipment needed. Choose two children to liaise with the kitchen staff if some of this equipment is to be borrowed from them. Decide who will be responsible for bringing any extra items: tablecloths, flowers, vases, napkins.

See recipe for lemonade on page 44

School Cafés

THE MENU
What will you sell?
Will some children be able to bake some items at home?
What will be made at school?
What drinks will be sold? (If tea and coffee are served, it is necessary to enlist the help of parents.)

PUBLICITY
For the café to succeed you need customers. Decide who will be invited, and discuss how to publicise the event. You may decide on:-
- announcements in assembly (written and read by the children)
- two children to go around the classrooms with messages
- letters home to the parents composed by the children
- individual letters to special guests.

THEMES
A theme is not necessary but can give a focus.
Sometimes it can be related to a class project.
Some suggestions:-

A CLOWN CAFE
- You could perhaps invite a children's clown to come and perform a short act at one café, in exchange for giving out cards advertising his/her act to the parents.
- Menus and posters can be decorated with colourful clowns.
- The children may be dressed as clowns and act as waiters.
- Cakes and biscuits can be decorated with clown faces.

Costumes for the waiters at the Clown Café

Corner of a classroom or hall set up as a French café

A FRENCH CAFE
- Serve hot chocolate, croissants, pain au chocolat, open sandwiches on French bread.
- Hang French flags around the room.
- Waiters and waitresses can wear blue and white striped t-shirts and berets.
- Write the menu in French.
- Label the food in French.
- Teach the children a few French phrases.
- Collect posters advertising French food from a delicatessen.

AMERICAN DINER
- Sell milkshakes, brownies and other cookies, muffins, homemade lemonade, pizzas, potato skins etc. (See recipes on next page.)
- Waiters can wear baseball caps.
- Decorate the room with American flags.
- Play American rock music.

MONSTER CAFE
- Sell green jelly, monsters' eyes (grapes with Smarties pressed in), 'blood' (lemonade coloured red).
- Make up gruesome names for the food and design suitable labels.
- Children can wear masks or face paints.
- Decorate menus/posters with monster drawings using luminous pens, glitter, gold and silver.

There are limitless themes that can be used for the café, some connected to seasons or festivals: Easter, St. Valentine's Day, Hallowe'en, Guy Fawkes etc. If you decide not to have a theme it is still possible to make the café attractive with tablecloths, flowers, pretty menus etc. Live music adds to the atmosphere: recorders, piano music, violins etc.

School Cafés

FOOD AND DRINK
Hot drinks require adult help and supervision.

MULLED APPLE JUICE
Use concentrated apple juice. Dilute with hot water. Add cinnamon sticks, cloves and brown sugar to taste. Add sliced lemons, oranges and apples.

AMERICAN BROWNIES
Makes approximately 30 squares

225g (8oz) butter
400g (14oz) soft brown sugar
4 beaten eggs
225g (8oz) self-raising flour

75g (3oz) cocoa
a pinch of salt
milk

Beat butter and sugar until creamy. Gradually add the eggs. Mix flour, cocoa and salt, and fold into creamed mixture. Add enough milk to give a soft mixture. Bake in a greased and lined rectangular tin at 375°F/190°C (Gas Mark 5) for approx 25 minutes. Allow to cool, then cut into squares. (Chocolate icing can be added.)

CHEESY CRUNCHIES
Makes approximately 24 pieces

300g (11oz) soft margarine
300g (11oz) plain flour

300g (11oz) grated Cheddar cheese
200g (7oz) peanuts

Mix fat, flour and cheese thoroughly. Press into a greased baking tray. Cover with nuts and press lightly. Cut into fingers. Bake for 15-20 minutes in preheated oven at 350°F/180°C (Gas Mark 4)

EYEBALLS
Slit a seedless grape and add a red Smartie. (The colour runs and makes the 'eye' look bloodshot!)

MUFFINS
Makes approximately 20 muffins
2 eggs
175ml (6fl oz) milk
1 tablespoon vegetable oil
225g (8oz) self-raising flour
50g (2oz) sugar

Beat the eggs and add the milk and oil. In another bowl mix the flour and sugar together. Make well in the flour mixture and pour in liquid. Mix well. Spoon into small bun tins and bake in hot oven at 400°F/200°C (Gas Mark 6) for 10-15 minutes. The following can be added: chopped nuts/raisins/sultanas/glacé cherries or grated cheese with chopped onion/fresh or dried herbs.

POTATO SKINS
Bake potatoes in their jackets in a very hot oven. When fairly well cooked, remove from oven, carefully cut in half and scoop out most, but not all, of the middle. Brush the insides of the skins with oil and return them to the hot oven for 15 minutes or until crisp. You can fill these with dips such as sour cream and chives or crumbled crispy bacon.

Healthy Lunch Boxes

Some examples of healthy lunches

Discussion

Some questions to ask - Why do we need food? Do animals need food? Do plants need food?

FOOD FOR ENERGY

Everything we do needs energy. Energy in food is measured in kilojoules (kj.) or kilocalories (kcal.). If we take in more energy than we use we gain weight. Some foods are high in kj. or kcal. Collect labels from a variety of foods and see how many kilocalories there are in an average helping. Make diagrams to show how much of various foods adds up to 500 kcals., e.g. How many bags of crisps? How many apples?

How many kilocalories you use depends on how big and active you are, how old you are, on your sex, and your metabolic rate. About half the kilocalories you eat are used for physical activity like running, walking, cycling, even sitting. The other half are used for growth, breathing, digestion, etc. Which do you think uses the most kilocalories; skipping, running, jumping, standing still, walking? Do each of these for a few minutes to help you decide. Could you continue doing these for a long time?

FOOD FOR GROWTH AND REPAIR

Your body is made up of millions of cells. These are constantly dying and being replaced. The dust in a bedroom is mainly dead skin cells. All the material for new cells comes from food. Food is made up of lots of different things. For your body to grow properly you need different *nutrients*. Nutrients have different jobs in looking after our bodies. They work together to keep us healthy. The main nutrients are shown on the following page.

Healthy Lunch Boxes

NUTRIENTS

CARBOHYDRATES	– **give us energy**
Starches	● bread, potatoes, pasta, rice, cereals, flour
Sugars	● sugar, sweets, cakes (too many of these decay teeth and make us overweight)

PROTEINS	– **for growth and repair of our bodies**
Animal	● meat, fish, eggs, milk, cheese, yoghurt
Plant	● nuts, beans,grains, wheat, rice, lentils

FATS	– **give us energy, insulate and protect our bodies**
Animal	● meat, milk (full cream), cream, butter, cheese, eggs
Plant	● sunflower, corn, olive, soya oil etc. Too many of these make us fat. Too many animal fats can cause heart disease.

VITAMINS	– **help our bodies work properly**
	A - carrots, eggs, milk, oily fish - for growth, eyesight, throat
	B - cereals, milk, meat - for energy, nerves
	C - green vegetables, fruit - keep skin healthy, heal cuts, help to resist infection
	D - milk, butter, oily fish, liver - for strong bones and teeth
	E - wheatgerm, nuts, seeds, vegetable oils - for circulation, heart, skin

MINERALS	– **help bodies work and help growth**
	Calcium - milk, flour, green vegetables, fish - for strong bones and teeth
	Iron - red meat, liver, green vegetables, cereals - for red blood cells

FIBRE	– **prevents constipation**
	● wholemeal bread,wholemeal cereals, bran, raw fruit and vegetables

If you are short of some of these nutrients you can become ill. In the l8th Century sailors who were on the sea for a long time did not have any fresh fruit or vegetables, and many died of scurvy. This is an illness caused through a lack of Vitamin C. You need Vitamin D for strong bones. Some ancient Egyptians did not eat enough Vitamin D and their skeletons show they had bent bones. This condition was called rickets. Also, if you have *too much* of some foods (i.e. sugars, salt and fats) or not enough fruit, vegetables and fibre, you can become ill. Too much animal fat is bad for you. There is a lot of hidden fat in some foods. Carry out the following test to see whether the food has any fat in it.

TESTING FOR FATS

Put a selection of foods on a tray. Ask the children to predict which foods they think will have fat in them and, of those, which have more fat than others. Try cheese, peanuts, chocolate, butter and margarine. Rub or drop a small quantity of food onto squares of sugar paper. When dry, hold the paper to the light. The more fat in the sample, the more light will shine through. After the test, see how accurate the predictions were.

Pictures cut from magazines - 'Foods I should eat more of'

LUNCH BOX FOOD

Ask children to discuss the contents of lunch boxes. By checking with the nutrients list, see which nutrients are present in some typical lunch boxes. Which *nutrients* are best eaten in moderation? Therefore, which *foods* are best eaten in moderation?

Cut out pictures from magazines of various foods. Do not glue down instantly. Ask children which of the foods in the pictures they like and eat lots of, and which they do not like. Check from this whether they have a taste for healthy food or not. Ask each child to make two lists, one headed 'Foods I must eat less of' and one headed 'Foods I must eat more of'. (See photograph above.)

Ask children to suggest foods for a healthy lunch box. Here are some examples:-

PASTA / RICE

Choose a selection of fresh diced vegetables (cucumber, celery, green peppers, mushrooms, spring onions, apples, nuts, sultanas etc.) and add to cold cooked rice or pasta. Add a spoonful of dressing or mayonnaise.

Healthy Lunch Boxes

HEALTHY SANDWICH FILLINGS

Use wholemeal bread - (fibre and Vitamin B)

Carrot spread: Grate a carrot and some cheese (about one tablespoon). Mix together with a little mayonnaise.

Fishy filling: Chop 2 tomatoes. Mix in 2 tablespoons of tinned fish (sardine, tuna or pilchards).

Fruit delight: Grate an apple. Mix with a mashed banana. Add juice from half a lemon and I teaspoon of honey.

Curried fish: Add 2 chopped hard-boiled eggs to one tin of sardines. Mix with 1 tablespoon mayonnaise, 1 tablespoon lemon juice and half teaspoon curry powder.

Peanut butter and yeast extract: Spread the bread with a thin layer of yeast extract, and then a layer of peanut butter.

Cottage cheese spread: Add 2 tablespoons of chopped walnuts and 2 tablespoons of chopped apricots to a 225g pot of cottage cheese.

Spicy chicken: Mix diced chicken, mayonnaise and a pinch of cumin seeds, paprika powder, curry powder and turmeric.

Cheesy apple filling: Mix equal quantities of grated cheese and grated apple. Stir in a little lemon juice and some sultanas.

 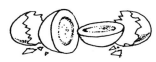  

Add to your lunch box some crunchy sticks: cucumber, celery, carrots, peppers, cauliflowers: all cut into sticks of bite-sized pieces.

HOMEMADE LEMONADE (full of Vitamin C)

4 lemons
l75g (6oz) caster sugar
900ml (I½ pt) water

Wash lemons and squeeze. Pour boiling water over skins. Stir in sugar, and leave to cool. Strain the water. Add lemon juice.

SAVOURY FLAN

Make shortcrust pastry from
225g (8oz) plain wholemeal flour
l00g (4oz) soft margarine
Water to bind
Filling: choice of vegetables (e.g. sliced tomatoes, sliced peppers, cooked leeks etc.)
4 eggs
l tablespoon milk
grated cheese

Mix the flour and margarine, and add the water. Roll out the pastry, and use it to line a flan dish. Give children a choice of the vegetables for filling. Fill the flan case with whichever combination they like. Beat the eggs and milk together, and pour this over the vegetables. Sprinkle with grated cheese. Bake for 40-45 minutes at 350°F/l80°C (Gas Mark 4).

DIGESTING YOUR FOOD

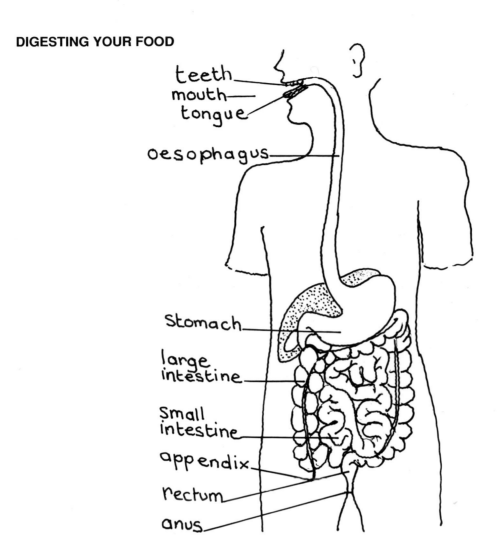

teeth
mouth
tongue
oesophagus
Stomach
large intestine
Small intestine
appendix
rectum
anus

Digesting your food means breaking it down into molecules which can be absorbed by the body.

Give the children a diagram of the human body, showing the organs that are used to digest food:

Mouth - teeth, saliva to make it easy to swallow.
Oesophagus - to send it along to the stomach.
Stomach - gastric juices begin digestion and break food down.
Duodenum (top of small intestine) - digestive juices from pancreas and gall bladder continue digestion.
Ileum (rest of small intestine) - produces more juices to aid digestion and begins absorption of released nutrients.
Colon (large intestine) - to process waste and absorb more minerals and water.
Rectum - waste collects here.
Anus - waste leaves body through the anus.

Make a life-sized coloured collage of the body digesting food. Label all the organs used in food digestion.

Sugar and Spice and all Things Nice

People have always craved sweet foods.

Test the class with two tastes - one sweet and one savoury (e.g. small piece of shortbread and piece of cheese) to see which they prefer. Count the numbers in each group. Point out that too much sugar is bad for people and can cause tooth decay, obesity and maybe some illnesses, so no-one should eat too much.

HONEY

History

- To satisfy their craving for sweet foods, people used to raid the nests of wild bees for honey. This is still practised in some parts of the world today. Wild bees deposit honey in crevices in rocks or tree trunks.
- Later people learned to attract bees into hives so that they could harvest the honey.
- The ancient Egyptians were probably the first beekeepers. As early as 4000 BC, Egyptians used honey for making sweets by mixing it with figs, dates, nuts and spices.
- They also used it for embalming. Alexander the Great was buried in coatings of honey.
- In Burma, all bodies were steeped in honey to preserve them until the money could be found for the funeral. When the funeral took place the honey was scraped off and sold in the market.
- Honey has a reputation for being valuable in repairing damaged skin and as a beauty preparation.
- Roman soldiers carried honey in their packs for treating their wounds.

TO MAKE A FACE PACK
Mix I tablespoon honey with I tablespoon lemon juice.
Spread over face and leave for ten minutes.

TO MAKE HAND LOTION
Mix I dessertspoon honey
I dessertspoons glycerine
2 tablespoons witch hazel
2 tablespoons vegetable oil
2 tablespoons warm water
I tablespoon fine oatmeal

Ask for volunteers to try the above potions.

Woodchip paper used for background; painted hive; tissue and cut-paper flowers; toilet roll bees; hexagon-shaped sponge for printed border

BEESWAX
● Beeswax is produced from special glands under a bee's body. From it are made the honeycombs that contain the eggs and the honey. The honeycombs are a hexagon shape. Draw hexagons - cut them out and see how they tessellate, as they do in the hive.

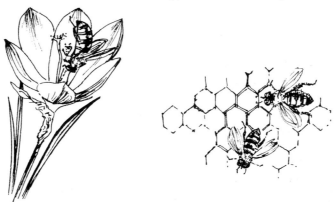

● The Roman Catholic Church has always used beeswax in its candles.
● Madame Tussaud's models are made from 75% beeswax to give the right colour to the skin.
● To produce 1lb of wax, a bee has to eat 5-l0lb of honey.

Sugar and Spice and all Things Nice

BEE-KEEPING

There are three kinds of bees in a hive:-

I. The Queen: She lays up to 3,000 eggs a day in summer. She does no work and is fed and groomed by other bees. If the queen leaves the hive all the bees follow her. The bee-keeper can lose all his bees in this way.

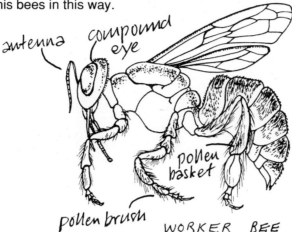

antenna   compound eye   pollen basket   pollen brush   WORKER BEE

2. Drones: These are the male bees, and very lazy. They are looked after by the worker bees, then fly out to meet and mate with a queen.

3. Workers: These are female bees, and very hard-working. They live for about six weeks, and build the combs from wax. Worker bees go from flower to flower sucking up nectar which they store in their honey stomachs. They put the nectar into the wax cells

Each worker bee makes 2,000 visits to flowers to produce one thimbleful of honey. To show other bees the direction in which the nectar can be found, worker bees dance a special figure of eight dance in the hive.

Art

Make bees out of toilet rolls with black and yellow paper used for the body, and white tissue wings and head. Hang bees in front of a picture of a beehive (see photograph).

Story

The Queen Bee by the Brothers Grimm.

Recipe

HONEY YOGHURT

Mix a large carton of natural goat's yoghurt with 2 tablespoons of honey. Add any of the following: chopped nuts, grated lemon or orange rind, sliced bananas or apple, sultanas, chopped dried apricots.

Eat it in class, or make larger portions and let each child take some home in a small yoghurt carton.

Cardboard house decorated with collage sweets; dough model of witch
(see Art/Technology on page 50)

SUGAR

History

● For thousands of years honey was all that people had to sweeten their food.

● Around l000 BC sugar cane was used in India for sweetness. People chewed the stalks of this plant to get out the syrup. Around 500 BC people in India learned how to make the syrup into sugar crystals.

● Sugar came to Europe in the 8th Century and by l3l9 was being imported to London. It was very expensive, costing about £20 for one pound in weight of sugar, so only the very wealthy people could afford it. Once they had tasted sugar the rich people wanted more. They sent explorers to faraway lands to search for sugar.

● By the l6th Century sugar products were considered essential items at Elizabethan banquets. It was made into fruit tarts, marmalade, marchpane (marzipan), sugar-bread, florentines, gingerbread etc.

● Queen Elizabeth I ate so much sugar her teeth became decayed and black.

● The sugar dishes at a banquet were made by a special sugar cook. Sometimes the wives of noblemen did their own sugar cooking.

● Sugar was also used to preserve food. Fruits and flowers were candied in sugar.

Sugar and Spice and all Things Nice

CANDY, CAKES AND PIES

- The first candy-making machine was invented in 1840. Candy was made in the form of a stick.

- The first lollipop was invented in 1890. Someone had the idea of putting a blob of candy on a stick and letting it harden.

- Ancient civilisations made cakes for their gods. Ancient Egyptians made it in the form of animals and birds.

- Now there are hundreds of different types of cakes. Let the children list some of the cakes they know.

- Pumpkin and apple pies are particularly popular in America. In New England apple pie is served frequently, sometimes even for breakfast.

DANISH ORANGE CAKE

100g (4oz) caster sugar
100g (4oz) margarine
100g (4oz) self-raising flour
2 eggs

Sauce:
2 oranges
1 lemon
50g (2oz) sugar

Grease a 20cm (8inch) cake tin. Cream together the sugar and margarine. Beat eggs and add to mixture. Fold in the flour and pour into the cake tin. Bake the mixture for 20 minutes at 375°F/190°C (Gas Mark 5).

Sauce: Squeeze the juice of the oranges and lemons. Add the sugar and boil until syrupy. Leave the cake in the tin and pour the syrup over the top. Leave the cake for a few days before eating, if possible.

Activities
- Make a tuck shop with lots of jars and boxes containing play food. This could be made from papier mâché, playdough or Plasticine.
- Make a list of all the different foods and their prices.
- Provide scales for weighing.
- What is the shop called?

This provides the opportunity for counting, weighing and money experience.

Art / Technology
Make gingerbread house from cardboard. Paint white, and decorate with sweets made from Cellophane wrapped around corks. Drinking straws, sweet papers, milk bottle tops etc. can be used to embellish the walls (see photograph on previous page).

GINGER

Where did the gingerbread man run? Who did he meet?

The Gingerbread Man.

The Gingerbread Man: characters made from cereal boxes (see Art on following page)

THE GINGER PLANT

Show children some ground ginger powder. Let them smell, touch and taste. Then show them some root ginger to compare. Discuss where they come from. Explain that they come from ginger plants. The 'root' ginger really comes from the underground stem of the ginger plant called a rhizome: it is not a true root. The stem of the ginger plant is often crystallised. When the ginger plant is a year old it is dug up and its thick rootlike parts are cut off, washed and dried in the sun. These knobbly roots are put into boiling water and peeled. They are then left to bleach to a pale brown colour in the sun. Ground ginger is made from these dried rhizomes. Ginger is grown in Africa, the West Indies and South America.

History
● For thousands of years people have been using the spice ginger.
● A Greek baker is supposed to have made the first gingerbread about 5000 years ago.
● The recipe for gingerbread was brought to the British Isles by the Romans.
● In medieval England, spices played an important part in the dishes of rich people. Ginger was cheaper than some spices but was still kept locked in the special spice chest. Ginger was added to stews, cakes, biscuits and even wine.
● London was the centre of the spice trade. It was controlled by the 'Guild of Pepperers'. This board was later called the 'Guild of Grocers' because they dealt with large quantities, which, in French, is 'en gros'. This is where the name 'grocers' for our local food shop comes from.
● Monks made gingerbread in monasteries. Instead of baking it plain, they cut it into fancy shapes: flowers, birds, animals, letters of the alphabet, people.
● Queen Elizabeth I gave a banquet at her palace and gave each of her guests a gingerbread figure that was a portrait of him/herself.

Language
Discuss what grocers sell today. List the names of other types of shops: hardware, chemists, haberdashers, milliners. Use an etymological dictionary to find out why they are so called.

Sugar and Spice and all Things Nice

The following is a good recipe for making biscuits in different shapes.

GINGERBREAD
Makes approximately 8 shapes

50g (2oz) margarine
50g (2oz) brown sugar
1 tablespoon golden syrup

Melt these ingredients in a pan and then pour into a bowl. Add:-

175g (6oz) plain flour
1 teaspoon ginger powder
Stir all ingredients together and roll out to 1/2 cm thickness. Cut into shapes. Cook for 20 minutes at 350°F/180°C (Gas Mark 4).

Shape cutters may be bought in metal or plastic. These days they come in all shapes and sizes. There are pigs, hearts, angels, ducks, stars etc.
You can also make your own from card. Use strong card and keep the shapes simple.

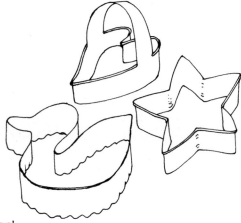

Story
'The Gingerbread Man'

Art
The above story lends itself to a wall display. This can be treated as an introduction to map-making, using models on a flat surface before wall-mounting (see photograph on page 51).

The following is a savoury recipe using ginger:

GINGER STIR-FRY VEGETABLES
A selection of onions, mushrooms, green peppers, carrots, courgettes, celery.
1 teaspoon of cumin seed   1 tablespoon soya sauce
25g (1oz) butter or oil   1 tablespoon lemon juice
2.5cm (1 inch) fresh root ginger

Slice the vegetables and add the cumin seed. Fry the mixture in the butter. Add the peeled and finely chopped ginger. Stir in the soya sauce and lemon juice. Fry on a low heat for 15 minutes, stirring occasionally. This makes a good filling for warm pitta bread.

CHOCOLATE

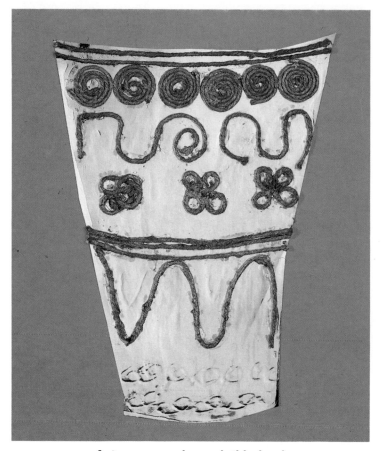

Aztecs served xocolatl in beakers

Aztec design with cacao tree

History
DRINKING CHOCOLATE

● Chocolate was first introduced into Europe by Cortez, a Spanish adventurer. He sailed to Mexico where the Emperor Montezuma gave him a drink called xocolatl. The Aztecs made this drink by roasting and grinding the seeds of the cacao tree and adding water, spices and vanilla. It was then stirred vigorously with a wooden swizzle stick to make it foamy. They served it in golden drinking vessels. The Spaniards conquered the Aztecs, stole their treasures and took back bags full of the cacao seeds. The Aztecs drank their chocolate very thick and bitter, but the Spaniards added sugar and honey to make it sweeter.

● Slowly the craze for the chocolate drink spread to the rest of Europe. People believed it had great healing powers and provided stamina and good health. It was a very expensive drink and only the rich could afford to buy it.

● Chocolate came to England in the l650's. It was mainly available in 'chocolate houses'. People visited them in their best clothes, and drank the strong drink together.

● Later the drink was made with milk instead of water.

● Chocolate is rich in iron and calcium and also contains protein, fat and carbohydrates - a compact source of nutrients usefully included in rations taken on expeditions.

Sugar and Spice and all Things Nice

THE CACAO TREE

The cacao tree is rather unusual. It has a silvery trunk and large shiny green leaves about 25-30cm long. New leaves appear all year round. They are soft and pink when new. The blossoms also grow all year round. They have five pink and white petals and grow right out of the trunk. The cacao pods also grow directly from the trunk. They are about 20cm long and some pods are green to start with, and then turn yellow. Others begin dark red and turn to scarlet.

Recipes

AZTEC CHOCOLATE

To make xocolatl like the Aztecs drank it, mix 2 teaspoons cocoa with 4 teaspoons water. Stir it into a smooth paste. Add a cup of cold water and a few drops of vanilla essence. Whisk the mixture until it is foamy. Add some ground black pepper. Let the children sip the mixture to see if they like it.

HOT CHOCOLATE

Make some hot chocolate as we drink it now with hot milk and sugar. Compare the taste with xocolatl.

Art

Make a collage cacao tree.

CHOCOLATE BARS

History

- In the early l800's a Dutchman invented a press to take out the fat from the cocoa beans. This cocoa butter formed the basis for eating chocolate.
- In l876 a Swiss man added milk to chocolate and made milk chocolate. Nestlé and Lindt started producing chocolate bars.
- In l905 Cadbury's made their first Dairy Milk bar.
- In the l930's many variations to the chocolate bar were made: Crunchie, Mars Bars, Black Magic, Aeros, Maltesers, Kit-Kats, Rolos, Smarties.

See Maths below

Maths
Carry out a survey of children's favourite chocolate bars. Make a block graph to show which are the most popular. Glue the wrapping papers of the different chocolates in the columns of the graph.

Writing
Letters to different chocolate manufacturers will result in a wealth of posters and information about their products.

Technology
- Invent your own chocolate.
- Ask the children to invent their own chocolate bar. Describe it in detail: its shape, contents, taste etc.
- Invent a name for the new bar.
- Design its wrapping.
- Study chocolate advertisements and write your own advertisement for your bar.
- Design posters to advertise the new bars.
- Make 'sculptures' of chocolates and boxes.
- Design and make boxes that open, with sweets inside made from papier mâché, Plasticine, cloth, or any other suitable material.

Art
- Look at the work of the artist Claes Oldenberg who makes 'soft' sculptures of food. Make big models of chocolates using a variety of cloths. Glue or sew, and stuff with newspaper. These can be very decorative, using taffeta, gold lamé and other glittery and shiny materials.

Sugar and Spice and all Things Nice

Recipes

CHOCOLATE CHIP COOKIES
Makes approximately 40 cookies
250g (9oz) margarine
l00g (4oz) soft brown sugar
2 eggs
250g (9oz) plain flour
l teaspoon baking powder
100g (4oz) chocolate chips

Beat together margarine, sugar and eggs. Sift in the flour and baking powder. Stir in chocolate chips. Grease a baking tray. Add drops of the mixture onto the tray (leaving room for them to spread). Bake in a preheated oven 375°F/l90°C (Gas Mark 5) for 8-l0 minutes. Cool on a wire rack.

CHOCOLATE CHEWS
Makes approximately 20
150g (5oz) margarine
150g (5oz) castor sugar
75g (3oz) dessicated coconut
150g (5oz) self-raising flour
65g (2 ½ oz) crushed cornflakes
4 level tablespoons cocoa powder or drinking chocolate powder
Icing
175g (6oz) icing sugar
2 tablespoons cocoa or drinking chocolate powder
4 tablespoons milk

Heat the oven to 350°F/180°C (Gas Mark 4). Grease a shallow tin (about 28cm x 18cm). Melt the margarine in a saucepan. Remove from heat. Stir in all the other ingredients and press evenly into a tin. Bake for 15-20 minutes. Remove from the oven and leave to cool. Cut into fingers. Blend the ingredients to make icing and spread over the fingers.

CHOCOLATE CRACKLE CAKES
Makes approximately 9 cakes

50g (2oz) sugar	2 tablespoons golden syrup
50g (2oz) butter	50g (2oz) cornflakes
2 tablespoons cocoa	

Melt the sugar, butter and cocoa together in a saucepan over a low heat. Add the golden syrup. Take care the mixture does not boil. Remove from heat and add cornflakes. Stir until the cornflakes are coated with the mixture. Put small piles into cake cases and leave to set.

N.B. It should be explained that chocolate is high in calories, containing large amounts of fat and sugar, and is all right to enjoy occasionally but not too often. A calorie count of the above recipe could be compared to that for a *low* calorie recipe, e.g. apple scones.

The Science of Cookery

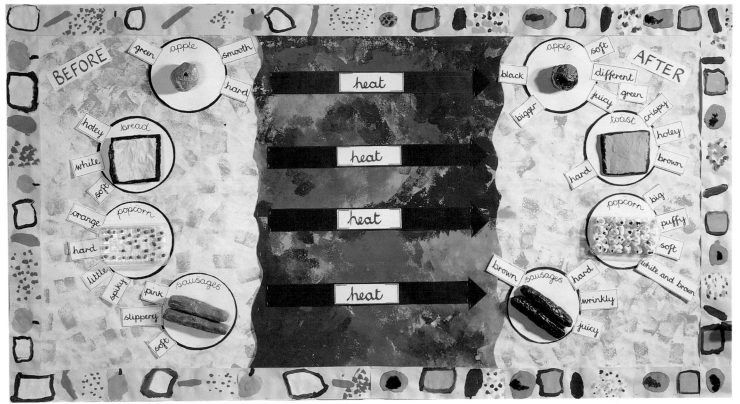

A classroom display showing changes to foods when cooked

Changes occur in cookery when there is an alteration of temperature, or liquid is added to a substance, or different substances are mixed together. There are many examples of such changes. Children can be made aware of this aspect of the subject by the teacher encouraging the children:

1. to closely observe the processes involved in cooking and the changes that they produce
2. to predict what changes will occur during cooking
3. to measure, describe and record before and after a change has taken place
4. to hypothesise on why the changes have taken place.

To practise these scientific processes, try the following activities:-

MAKING TOAST
Cut a slice of white bread. Ask the children to consider the following:-
● What does the bread taste like?
● What colour is the bread?
● Does it smell?
● What does it weigh?
● Measure the length, width and thickness of the slice of bread.
● Describe its texture.

The answers may be given orally or written in a descriptive passage or recorded on a chart.
Ask the children to predict what will happen if the bread is exposed to heat (in a toaster or under a grill). Ask them what they think will change. **Toast the bread. Describe how it has changed.**

The Science of Cookery

Ask the children to hypothesise on
- why it has shrunk
- why it has lost weight
- why it has changed colour
- why the texture has changed.

Let the children taste the toast. Ask them if they prefer the taste before or after the bread was toasted.
Put another slice of toast in the toaster and let it burn. Show how more heat changes the bread to a darker colour which demonstrates that more carbon has formed.

Ask the children to follow the same processes of observation, prediction, recording and hypothesising when observing the changes that occur in the following activities:-

● grilling sausages
● baking an apple
● boiling an egg
● making an iced lolly from blackcurrant juice

COOKING POPCORN
This is a popular activity as the change that takes place is quick and dramatic and produces something good to eat. The change occurs through **expansion** of the moisture inside the corn which turns to steam when the corn is heated, and bursts through the skin. To demonstrate this, put a handful of hard, yellow corn in a heavy bottomed pan with a tablespoonful of oil. Place over a moderate heat. Within minutes, the corn will expand and jump around the pan. The corn turns into a light, soft substance which has lost its colour and turned white. It is delicious when served plain, or with melted butter and salt.

MICROBES IN COOKING

YOGHURT
Very small living creatures are necessary to make yoghurt. They are called **bacteria**. Bacteria are **microscopic** organisms which feed on and **excrete** into the milk. This makes the milk turn sour and it turns into yoghurt.

Vocabulary
Bacteria - microscopic organisms (very tiny living creatures)
Excrete - to put out unwanted material from the body

TO MAKE YOGHURT
Mix 425g (l5oz) tin of evaporated milk with enough water to make a pint. Add a tablespoonful of 'live' yoghurt i.e. yoghurt with live bacteria. Heat the liquid to blood temperature - 37°C (dip a finger in and it should feel the same temperature). Keep it at this heat for twelve hours. The easiest way is to pour it into a Thermos flask. If left overnight, the milk will have turned into thick yoghurt. It is important that the mixture is neither too hot nor too cold as the bacteria need the correct temperature to live and reproduce.

Discussion
Ask the children to recall other changes that they have observed during the process.

Follow up
Find out about Louis Pasteur and the pasteurisation of milk.

One Potato, Two Potato...

Map showing the geographical and historical aspects of potatoes

History

Potatoes were an important part of the diet of people from the Andes Mountains. They found small potatoes growing wild in the valleys between the mountains. This was 2,500 years ago. Later they learned how to cultivate them. During the l6th Century some Spanish explorers found people of the Andes eating flat baked potato cakes. They liked the flavour of them so they took some potato tubers home.

Potatoes were introduced into Britain in the 16th Century by explorers who discovered them at about the same time as the Spanish. At first they were not popular in Britain, and in Scotland a law was passed to forbid the growing of potatoes. They were thought to be unholy because they belong to the deadly nightshade family. However, potatoes were very popular in Ireland and soon became the staple food of the Irish. There was a great deal of poverty in Ireland and potatoes proved a cheap and nourishing food supply. A potato blight ruined the potato harvests in 1845, 1846 and 1848: overnight, potato fields were hit by the disease and healthy plants became black and rotting. Thousands of Irish people starved to death, others emigrated to Britain and America, and so the potato helped to change the face of history.

Language

There are many dialect words for potatoes. See how many you know: spuds, tatties, praties.
Make a list of all the different varieties of potatoes: King Edward, Maris Piper, Desirée, Cara, Romano, Pentland Crown, Epicure, Home Guard, Record, Arran Pilot.

Maths

Make a block graph to show how the children prefer their potatoes cooked. Make columns: baked, boiled, roasted, chipped, mashed. Leave wide columns for each category and let the children make a potato print in the column of their choice. Collate the results. Try the activity in another class and compare the results.

AMAZING POTATO FACTS

We eat six million tonnes of potatoes each year in Britain.
We spend £2,500,000,000 a year on potatoes.
We eat an average of 4½ bags of potato crisps,
per person each week.
Collect similar figures for the classroom.
How many potatoes are eaten each week by the class?
What do they cost? How many bags of crisps are eaten?

One Potato, Two Potato, Three Potato, Four

Art

Potatoes are excellent to print with. Cut the potatoes in half and cut a simple design. Paint the cut design and place in a repetitive pattern on paper. Potato-printed paper is attractive for wrapping paper, covering books or folders (see Christmas section, page 28).

Visits

If possible, arrange to visit a farm that grows potatoes. At any time of year there is something interesting to see.

DECEMBER - JANUARY - Seed potatoes are delivered from Scotland. They are left to grow shoots. The fields are ploughed.

FEBRUARY - APRIL - potatoes are planted.

APRIL - AUGUST - Some farmers spray the potato plants to guard against disease. Many farmers grow potatoes under tunnels of polythene to protect them from frost.

AUGUST - OCTOBER - A mechanical potato harvester digs and sorts the potatoes. Often the potato plant is burned off about two weeks before harvesting. This helps to improve the skins of the potatoes.

GROW YOUR OWN POTATOES

Potatoes are easy to grow and can be grown in an old dustbin if there is no land available at the school. It is very satisfying for children to harvest their own potatoes. Buy seed potatoes from a reliable source so that they are guaranteed to be free of disease. Let them sprout or 'chit' indoors. To do this, stand the potatoes in an egg box with its 'rose-end' (that is the end with the most eyes) facing upwards. Before planting, knock off all the shoots except the three largest. Make holes in the soil 15cm deep. Sow potatoes, with the sprouts pointing up, around the middle of March. Water well. As the potatoes grow, make mounds of earth to cover them, or cover with black plastic sheeting. After the plants have flowered, you can dig up the potatoes.

Recipes

BAKED POTATOES

Baked potatoes are easy to prepare and can have a variety of toppings. Scrub medium to large size potatoes. Rub the skins with cooking oil and sprinkle with salt. Prick with a fork. Bake in the middle of a moderately hot oven 375°F/190°C (Gas Mark 5) until soft when squeezed (about 1½ - 2 hours).**Toppings:** grated cheese, butter, cottage cheese, chopped ham, tuna fish, baked beans.

LEEK AND POTATO SOUP

Makes enough for everyone in the class to have a taste

450g (1lb) leeks	600ml (1pt) water
450g (1lb) potatoes	600ml (1pt) milk
25g (1oz) margarine	parsley, if available

Peel, wash and slice the vegetables. Sauté them gently in the melted margarine. Add the liquid and simmer for 20 to 30 minutes. Season to taste. You could push this mixture through a sieve to make a puréed soup.

SPANISH OMELETTE

1 onion - chopped	6 eggs
1 tablespoon olive oil	1 tablespoon parsley - chopped
450g (1lb) cold cooked potatoes	salt and pepper

Sauté the onion in the oil until soft. In a bowl beat together the egg, parsley, salt and pepper. Stir in the potato and onion. Pour this mixture into a pan and cook gently for 15 minutes. Place the omelette under the grill for a minute to brown. Serve hot or cold.

How Does Your Garden Grow?

Cress and bean sprouts grown in the classroom

GROW YOUR OWN FOOD

Growing food is particularly satisfying and does not require outdoor space. Any plants can be grown in containers as long as the containers are deep enough to support the root system. Be inventive and collect a variety of containers, some of which can be used in the classroom and others which can stand outside. Any of the following will be useful: pots, pans, kettles, baking trays, old drawers, bins, baths, baskets, toilets. Use a suitable potting compost, and crocks at the base to aid drainage.

FAST MOVERS

MUSTARD AND CRESS

Growing food usually takes time and requires patience. However, some seeds germinate very quickly and can be eaten within days. Mustard and cress is a favourite for this reason. The seeds just need moisture: damp blotting paper on a saucer will do. The children can 'sow' their own initials. Alternatively, more decorative containers can be used with the mustard and cress grown to resemble hair. Try eggshells (see photograph above), orange or grapefruit skins.

Rest the eggshell on a small card cylinder to stop it rolling, and decorate the eggshell with felt-tip pens or coloured paper. Orange and grapefruit skins can be made into faces with pieces of carrot, potato peeling, apple peeling, etc. attached with pins to make the features of a face. Damp cottonwool inside the containers is all that is needed on which to sow the seeds. Potatoes can also be used. Make holes in three or four potatoes with a cocktail stick. Push seeds in the holes. The moisture from the potato will be sufficient for the seeds to sprout. Join the potatoes together to make a 'monster'. Use cocktail sticks for joints and legs. When the mustard and cress grows the monster will appear to have green hair. It is easy to draw a face on potato skins with a black felt-tip pen.

Recipe

Mustard and cress make a good salad addition to sandwiches. Add to: cream cheese, egg and mayonnaise, cottage cheese, sardine, tuna and cucumber.

SPROUTING BEANS

Other salad vegetables that are quick to grow indoors are sprouting beans. The following sprout easily and are very nutritious:
- mung bean
- aduki beans
- chick peas

They sprout faster if they are left to soak in water overnight. Then rinse the seeds thoroughly. Put a tablespoonful of seeds into a jam jar. Cover the top of the jar with muslin and attach muslin with an elastic band. Leave the jar on its side in a warm place. Each day, wash the seeds by pouring warm water into the jar. Swill the seeds and pour out the water. Within a few days the seeds will start to sprout.

Handfuls of sprouting seeds can be added to soups, stews, green salads, rice dishes.

How Does Your Garden Grow?

GROW BAGS

Varieties of tomatoes, young tomato plants and cross-sectional drawings

Grow bags are ideal for growing vegetables inside the classroom as they arrive filled with potting compost. This is clean and disease-free and is the right texture for draining. Grow bags don't need drainage holes so they don't make a mess.

TOMATOES

Tomatoes grow particularly well in grow bags. A warm, sunny, light spot in the classroom is very like a greenhouse with just the right conditions for a good crop of tomatoes.

Tomato plants can be obtained from seed or grown on from small plants. The seeds should be sown in January about 5cm apart and just covered with compost. They only need to be watered sparingly. Germination will take 7-8 days. When two leaves have formed they should be thinned out. Larger plants need to be about 40cm apart. Tomato plants have to be watered frequently, but they don't like cold water which will cause 'chilling' and slow down their growth: so use lukewarm water.

Tomatoes grown indoors will not be pollinated by bees or wind, so they need help. Brushing each flower centre with a small brush or a few feathers tied to the end of a small stick will help the fruit to form. Spraying the plants lightly with water (not cold) will also assist with pollination.

The stems of the growing plants must always be supported with canes. You must always pinch out the side shoots which grow between the main stem and the leaf stalks. This concentrates the plant's energy into a single main stem. Once eight 'trusses' (flowerheads) have formed you should stop the plant growing any taller by pinching the main stem above the developing trusses.

Harvest the tomatoes as they are just about to turn red. Any green tomatoes that are not ripening can be put in a warm dark place (like a desk drawer) to redden.

Varieties

There are a number of varieties of tomatoes, all with lovely names. These differ from each other in size, shape and colour of the fruit. This will surprise some children who think a tomato is a tomato is a tomato. If they are making project books on food, they can cut out the pictures from catalogues and name them.

Maths
Recording of growth - at all stages encourage the children to record and describe the changes which they observe. This can be done by using charts to record height, number of leaves, number of flowers, length of leaves etc. Time, measurement and number work can all be involved.

Art
Draw the plants at regular intervals, looking closely at the shape of leaves, number of petals on the flowers, etc. Pastels on black paper look effective when the plants are in flower. Big colourful paintings of the plants with the bright fruit hanging from the stems look very cheerful. Cut open a tomato and draw a cross section in coloured pastels or crayons. Look at the seeds. Point out to the children the cycle involved: SEEDS TO PLANTS AND BACK TO SEEDS AGAIN.

Writing
Children need not simply record the growth of plants. They can describe the excitement, anticipation, pleasure, satisfaction, wonder and sometimes frustration involved in growing their tomato plants.

Vocabulary
Compost, germination, pollination, shoots, stems, stalks, flowerheads, ripen, redden, scarlet, blush, tinge.

Recipes
Fresh tomatoes smell and taste delicious so you may wish to eat them just as they are. The following recipes retain and enhance the fresh taste and also look pretty (see photograph opposite).

STUFFED TOMATOES
12 firm tomatoes
225g (8oz) fresh wholemeal breadcrumbs
225g (8oz) cream cheese
4 tablespoons finely chopped spring onions
salt and pepper to taste

Wash and dry the tomatoes. Cut a 'lid' from the top of each. Gently scoop out the pulp. Chop the pulp and add the breadcrumbs, cream cheese and onion. Mix well and season. Fill the tomatoes and replace the lids. Refrigerate until needed.

TOMATO AND CRESS SANDWICHES
For instant enjoyment of newly ripened tomatoes, sandwiches can be made, combining the chopped or sliced tomatoes with cress.

BRUSCHETTA
Toast some bread, spread with finely chopped tomatoes, and drizzle olive oil over the top. Season to taste. This is a delicious lunchtime or teatime snack.

How Does Your Garden Grow?

Stuffed tomatoes, and tomato and cress sandwiches

FRESH TOMATO SOUP
Plenty for a class to taste

l large onion, finely chopped	lKg (2lb) ripe chopped tomatoes
l large carrot, grated	pinch of mixed herbs
2 stalks celery, chopped	l ¼ litres (2 pts) vegetable stock
2 tablespoons margarine	l tablespoon tomato purée
salt and pepper	

Fry the onion, carrot and celery in the margarine. Add the tomatoes and herbs, then simmer for about l5 minutes. Add the stock and cook for about l0 minutes. Add the tomato purée, salt and pepper. Allow to cool slightly and then liquidise, or push the mixture through a sieve. Reheat before serving.

TOMATOES WITH YOGHURT AND BASIL
This can be used as a dip, or as a spread for toast

450g (llb) tomatoes	300ml (¼ pt) natural yoghurt
50g (2oz) butter	2 tablespoons chopped basil or parsley
salt and black pepper	25g (loz) pine kernels (optional)
pinch of sugar	

Chop tomatoes coarsely. Melt the butter in a shallow pan and cook the tomatoes gently for a few minutes. Remove the pan from the heat and add salt, pepper and sugar. Beat the yoghurt and stir into the pan. Stir in the chopped parsley and pour into serving dish. Scatter the pine kernels over the top.
Serve with pitta bread, toast or crackers.

MUSHROOMS

Mushrooms are very easy to grow from one of the pre-sown packs that are available from the garden centre. These come in buckets or plastic bags filled with compost and the mushroom 'spawn'. These kits have full instructions with them and are almost foolproof. Mushrooms produced in this way can be grown at any time of the year. They don't need light and therefore any odd corner of a storage cupboard will suffice. The only care they need is to be kept moist. When the **spawn** absorbs the moisture, the **mycelium** (rooting system) awakens from its dormant stage. The mushrooms are the fruiting head of the mycelium. They appear in bursts over a period of weeks and should be picked when the caps open up. Growing mushrooms in this way can lead to a project on **fungi.**

WARNING

If you are studying fungi with children do *stress* that while mushrooms are an edible kind of fungi, most fungi are not edible. Some would make you ill: some are deadly poisonous. **It is unwise to suggest to children that they identify mushrooms from a book and collect them from the countryside.**

FUNGI FACTS

Fungi do not produce their own food like plants. Instead they live off dead and decaying matter like leaf litter, rotting logs, dead trees, piles of manure, stale food. Some fungi live on and feed off living things such as trees and other plants. Fungi can be seen at any time of the year, especially if the weather has been warm and wet, but they are particularly prolific in Autumn. Unlike most plants, fungi do not need sunlight to survive. They can grow in complete darkness. There are many different kinds of fungi.

FUNGI FRUIT

Below ground a fungus is a mass of minute hair-like threads which penetrate organic matter on which the fungus is feeding. This network of threads is called the *mycelium*. The part of the plant body which we can see above ground is the fruit of the mycelium. The function of the fruit is to distribute thousands of spores. These are usually carried in the air and then new fungi may grow where they land.

PARTS OF A MUSHROOM

How Does Your Garden Grow?

Mushroom-growing kit; examples of different mushrooms; a mushroom salad

SPORE PRINTS

Place a mushroom cap, gills down, on a piece of paper. Leave overnight. Spores will be released onto the paper and will leave a print.

Art

Collect or buy a variety of different mushrooms. Arrange on plates and in baskets. Offer the children a wide range of different drawing materials: pastels, crayons, coloured pencils, pen and ink, charcoal, paint.

Examine the shape, structure and colour of the mushrooms closely. Do carefully-observed still life drawings in a variety of media. Paint will require mixing to try to match the subtle colours of the mushrooms. Touches of gold and silver paint or pen can help to achieve effective pictures. Other still life pictures can be attempted in collage. Rip suitably coloured tissue, crêpe paper, newspaper, sugar paper etc. and assemble to make collage mushrooms.

Recipes
MUSHROOM PATE

1 small onion	150ml (¼ pt) hot water
450g (1lb) mushrooms	juice of ½ lemon
50g (2oz) margarine	175g (6oz) breadcrumbs
¼ teaspoon ground nutmeg, salt and pepper	

Finely chop the onion and mushroom. Fry gently in margarine until soft. Soak breadcrumbs in hot water and add to mushroom mixture with lemon juice. Cook over gentle heat. Remove from heat and beat in the remaining ingredients. Garnish with raw mushroom slices. Eat on pieces of toast and crackers.

HERBS

Growing and studying herbs is particularly interesting as they have a long and important history of uses for a wide variety of purposes. There is much folklore associated with herbs and they occur in many songs, poems and stories.

Most herbs will grow in old tubs or pots. They smell good, look attractive and have multiple uses. They can be grown from seed, cuttings or from small plants.

Bring fresh and dried herbs into the classroom to show to the children. Let them smell and taste a range of different herbs: parsley, chives, basil, thyme, marjoram, lavender, coriander, marigolds.

Explain to the children that the definition of a herb is a plant whose seeds, leaves or flowers can be useful.

History

● Long before records were kept, herbs had been used for food and medicine. These herbs would have been picked from the fields and hedgerows. Only by trial and error would our ancestors have learned which plants were safe to eat and which were poisonous. There were probably some nasty accidents during their experiments.

● The first written account of herbal remedies appeared in Babylon in 2000 BC. Many herbs that we use today were included: bay, thyme, coriander.

● Try these ancient remedies with children:
  - Rub teeth with sage leaves to whiten them and to freshen the mouth.
  - Put crushed mint leaves on bruises.
  - Rub lemon balm, rosemary or mint on to nettle stings.

● The ancient Egyptians imported many herbs to use for medicines, cosmetics and perfumes. They also used them to dye clothes and in the process of embalming.

● The ancient Greeks and the Romans were enthusiastic herbalists. The Romans carried herbs with them as they conquered Europe, and planted seeds everywhere they went. They introduced about 200 herbs into Britain, including parsley, rosemary, sage, thyme.

● With the establishment of monasteries in the Middle Ages, herbal medicine became widespread. The monks tended neat, well-planned gardens and grew famous for their herbal healing methods.

● Later it was customary for the woman of the household to tend the herb garden. She decided which herbs to grow. She harvested the herbs and added them to her cooking, wines and cordials. Some she dried and made into pot-pourris and perfume sachets.

TO MAKE POMANDERS

Pomanders were carried by Elizabethan ladies. They held them under their noses to counteract the nasty smells of Elizabethan streets.

You will need:
a large orange
some cloves
a teaspoonful each of orris root, cinnamon powder, allspice

Use a skewer to make holes all over the orange. Push the cloves into the holes. They should be closely packed. Then roll the orange into the orris root mixture. Wrap the orange in tissue paper and leave in a dark cupboard for about four weeks. Tie ribbon around the pomander with a loop at the top so that it can be hung.

How Does Your Garden Grow?

Herbs which can be grown in pots on the classroom windowsill

Recipes

BASIL AND GARLIC VINEGAR

l clove garlic
l0 tablespoons chopped basil
450ml (¾ pint) white wine vinegar

Peel and chop the garlic. Add the chopped basil leaves and pound together. Stir these ingredients into the vinegar and pour into a bottle. Seal tightly and keep for two weeks, shaking every day. Strain and rebottle.

The same recipe can be used substituting tarragon, burnet, sage or thyme for basil. Tie a ribbon round the neck of the bottle, and make a colourful label. This would make an attractive gift.

YOGHURT AND MINT SAUCE

300ml (½ pint) natural yoghurt
l cucumber
l clove garlic
salt and pepper
24 mint leaves

Beat the yoghurt in a bowl. Peel the cucumber and grate coarsely. Peel and crush the garlic. Chop the mint leaves finely (scissors can be used). Mix all the ingredients.
This sauce suits many dishes: cold chicken, new potatoes, or as a dip for sliced raw vegetables.

notes

For sales and distribution outside America:

Folens Publishers, Albert House, Apex Business Centre,
Boscombe Road, Dunstable, Beds., LU5 4RL, England

For further details of Belair publications
please write to:-

Belair Publications Ltd.,
P. O. Box 12,
Twickenham,
TW1 2QL,
England

BELAIR PUBLICATIONS USA

116 Corporation Way
Venice, Florida 34292